HUMAN

EXPERIMENTATION

WHEN RESEARCH IS EVIL

IDEAS in CONFLICT

Gary E. McCuen

GARY McCUEN
publications inc.

411 Mallalieu Drive
Hudson, Wisconsin 54016
Phone (715) 386-7113

Illustration and Photo Credits

Jerry Fearing 23, 111, 169; President's Commission for the Study of Ethical Problems in Medicine and Biomedical and Behavioral Research 127, 149, 155, 163; Steve Sack 81; Trials of War Criminals before the Nuernberg Military Tribunals 13, 31; U.S. Army Report on Japanese Biological Warfare Activities 36; U.S. Department of Energy 137; U.S. Senate Committee on Veterans' Affairs 95.

© 1998 by Gary E. McCuen Publications, Inc.
411 Mallalieu Drive, Hudson, Wisconsin 54016

(715) 386-7113

International Standard Book Number
0-86596-144-1
Printed in the United States of America

CONTENTS

Ideas in Conflict

Chapter 1   THE MEDICAL EXPERIMENTS OF WORLD WAR II

Chapter 2   THE TUSKEGEE EXPERIMENT

Chapter 5	**RESEARCH AND ETHICS: THE PRINCIPLE OF INFORMED CONSENT**

REASONING SKILL DEVELOPMENT

These activities may be used as individualized study guides for students in libraries and resource centers or as discussion catalysts in small group and classroom discussions.

IDEAS
in CONFLICT

This series features ideas in conflict on political, social, and moral issues. It presents counterpoints, debates, opinions, commentary, and analysis for use in libraries and classrooms. Each title in the series uses one or more of the following basic elements:

Introductions that present an issue overview giving historic background and/or a description of the controversy.

Counterpoints and debates carefully chosen from publications, books, and position papers on the political right and left to help librarians and teachers respond to requests that treatment of public issues be fair and balanced.

Symposiums and forums that go beyond debates that can polarize and oversimplify. These present commentary from across the political spectrum that reflect how complex issues attract many shades of opinion.

A global emphasis with foreign perspectives and surveys on various moral questions and political issues that will help readers to place subject matter in a less culture-bound and ethnocentric frame of reference. In an ever-shrinking and interdependent world, understanding and cooperation are essential. Many issues are global in nature and can be effectively dealt with only by common efforts and international understanding.

Reasoning skill study guides and discussion activities provide ready-made tools for helping with critical reading and evaluation of content. The guides and activities deal with one or more of the following:

RECOGNIZING AUTHOR'S POINT OF VIEW

INTERPRETING EDITORIAL CARTOONS

VALUES IN CONFLICT

WHAT IS EDITORIAL BIAS?

WHAT IS SEX BIAS?

WHAT IS POLITICAL BIAS?

WHAT IS ETHNOCENTRIC BIAS?

WHAT IS RACE BIAS?

WHAT IS RELIGIOUS BIAS?

*From across **the political spectrum** varied sources are presented for research projects and classroom discussions. Diverse opinions in the series come from magazines, newspapers, syndicated columnists, books, political speeches, foreign nations, and position papers by corporations and nonprofit institutions.*

About the Editor

Gary E. McCuen is an editor and publisher of anthologies for libraries and discussion materials for schools and colleges. His publications have specialized in social, moral and political conflict. They include books, pamphlets, cassettes, tabloids, filmstrips and simulation games, most of them created from his many years of experience in teaching and educational publishing.

7

CHAPTER 1

THE MEDICAL EXPERIMENTS OF WORLD WAR II

READING

1

THE CRIMES OF THE NAZI MEDICAL ESTABLISHMENT

Brigadier General Telford Taylor

After the defeat of Germany in WWII, the Office of Military Government for Germany (U.S.) issued orders to create a Tribunal which convened in Nuremberg, Germany, "to hear such cases as may be filed by the Chief of Council for war crimes." Brigadier General Telford Taylor served as Chief of Council for the Prosecution and delivered what follows in his opening statement at Tribunal I against the 23 defendants in the "Doctors' Trial." The "Doctors' Trial" or "Medical Case," officially The United States of America vs. Karl Brandt, et al. (Case No. 1) was tried at the Palace of Justice in Nuremberg, December 9, 1946 - July 18, 1947.

■ **POINTS TO CONSIDER**

1. Why were German doctors tried for war crimes?

2. Describe the scope and scale of their crimes.

3. What was the purpose of the high-altitude experiments?

4. How was scientific knowledge advanced by the Nazi medical experiments?

Excerpted from the Opening Statement of Telford Taylor, "Doctors' Trial," **German Miliary Tribunals, Trials of War Criminals**: vol. 1: 27-74.

Mankind has not heretofore felt the need of a word to denominate the science of how to kill prisoners most rapidly and subjugate people in large numbers. For the moment we will christen this macabre science "thanatology," the science of producing death.

The defendants in this case are charged with murders, tortures, and other atrocities committed in the name of medical science. The victims of these crimes are numbered in the hundreds of thousands. A handful only are still alive; a few of the survivors will appear in this courtroom. But most of these miserable victims were slaughtered outright or died in the course of the tortures to which they were subjected.

For the most part they are nameless dead. To their murderers, these wretched people were not individuals at all. They came in wholesale lots and were treated worse than animals. They were 200 Jews in good physical condition, 50 Gypsies, 500 tubercular Poles, or 1,000 Russians. The victims of these crimes are numbered among the anonymous millions who met death at the hands of the Nazis and whose fate is a hideous blot on the page of modern history.

THE GUISE OF RESEARCH

A sort of rough pattern is apparent on the face of the indictment. Experiments concerning high altitude, the effect of cold, and the potability of processed sea water have an obvious relation to aeronautical and naval combat and rescue problems. The mustard gas and phosphorous burn experiments, as well as those relating to the healing value of sulfanilamide for wounds, can be related to air-raid and battlefield medical problems. It is well known that malaria, epidemic jaundice, and typhus were among the principal diseases which had to be combated by the German Armed Forces and by German authorities in occupied territories.

To some degree, the therapeutic pattern outlined above is undoubtedly a valid one, and explains why the Wehrmacht, and especially the German Air Force, participated in these experiments. Fanatically bent upon conquest, utterly ruthless as to the means or instruments to be used in achieving victory, and callous to the sufferings of people whom they regarded as inferior, the German militarists were willing to gather whatever scientific fruit these experiments might yield.

But our proof will show that a quite different and even more sinister objective runs like a red thread through these hideous researches. We will show that in some instances the true object of these experiments was not how to rescue or to cure, but how to destroy and kill. The sterilization experiments were, it is clear, purely destructive in purpose. The prisoners at Buchenwald who were shot with poisoned bullets were not guinea pigs to test an antidote for the poison; their murderers really wanted to know how quickly the poison would kill. This destructive objective is not superficially as apparent in the other experiments, but we will show that it was often there.

Mankind has not, heretofore, felt the need of a word to denominate the science of how to kill prisoners most rapidly and subjugate people in large numbers. This case and these defendants have created this gruesome question. For the moment we will christen this macabre science "thanatology," the science of producing death. The thanatological knowledge, derived in part from these experiments, supplied the techniques for genocide, a policy of the Third Reich, exemplified in the "euthanasia" program and in the widespread slaughter of Jews, gypsies, Poles, and Russians. This policy of mass extermination could not have been so effectively carried out without the active participation of German medical scientists.

HIGH-ALTITUDE EXPERIMENTS

The experiments known as "high-altitude" or "low-pressure" experiments were carried out at the Dachau concentration camp in 1942. The reports, conclusions, and comments on these experiments, which were introduced here and carefully recorded, demonstrate complete disregard for human life and callousness to suffering and pain. These documents reveal at one and the same time the medical results of the experiments, and the degradation of the physicians who performed them. The first report by Rascher was made in April 1942, and contains a description of the effect of the low-pressure chamber on a 37-year-old Jew. I quote:

"The third experiment of this type took such an extraordinary course that I called an SS physician of the camp as witness, since I had worked on these experiments all by myself. It was a continuous experiment without oxygen at a height of 12 kilometers conducted on a 37-year-old Jew in good general condition. Breathing continued up to 30 minutes. After four minutes the

11

experimental subject began to perspire and wiggle his head, after five minutes cramps occurred, between six and ten minutes breathing increased in speed and the experimental subject became unconscious; from 11 to 30 minutes breathing slowed down to three breaths per minute, finally stopping altogether. "Severest cyanosis developed in between and foam appeared at the mouth."

"At five minutes intervals electrocardiograms from three leads were written. After breathing had stopped, EKG (electrocardiogram) was continuously written until the action of the heart had come to a complete standstill. About 1/2 hour after breathing had stopped, dissection was started."

Rascher's report also contains the following record of the "autopsy":

"When the cavity of the chest was opened the pericardium was filled tightly (heart tamponade). Upon opening of the pericardium, 80 cc. of clear yellowish liquid gushed forth. The moment the tamponade had stopped, the right auricle of the heart began to beat heavily, at first at the rate of 60 actions per minute, then progressively slower. Twenty minutes after the pericardium had been opened, the right auricle was opened by puncturing it. For about 15 minutes, a thin stream of blood spurted forth. Thereafter, clogging of the puncture wound in the auricle by coagulation of the blood and renewed acceleration of the action of the right auricle occurred."

"One hour after breathing had stopped, the spinal marrow was completely severed and the brain removed. Thereupon, the action of the auricle of the heart stopped for 40 seconds. It then renewed its action, coming to a complete standstill eight minutes later. A heavy subarachnoid edema was found in the brain. In the veins and arteries of the brain, a considerable quantity of air was discovered. Furthermore, the blood vessels in the heart and liver were enormously obstructed by embolism."

After seeing this report Himmler ironically ordered that if a subject should be brought back to life after enduring such an experiment, he should be "pardoned" to life imprisonment in a concentration camp. Rascher's reply to this letter, dated 20 October 1942, reveals that up to the time the victims of these experiments had all been Poles and Russians, that some of them had been condemned to death, and Rascher inquired whether Himmler's benign mercy extended to Poles and Russians. A tele-

DOCUMENT NO-610, PROSECUTION EXHIBIT 41

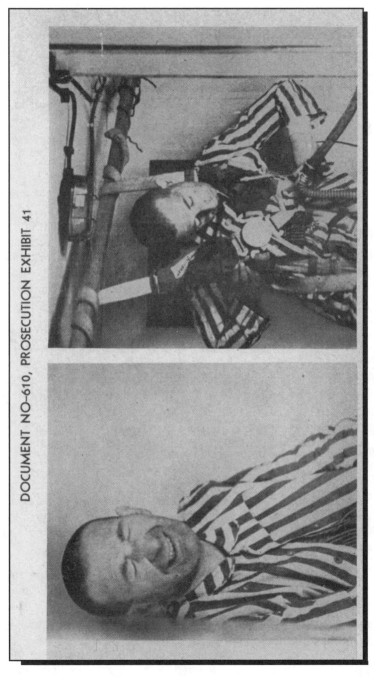

Source: "Doctors' Trial," **Germany Military Tribunals, Trials of War Criminals:** Vol. I: 27-74. Dec. 9, 1946-July 18, 1947

typed reply from the defendant, Rudolf Brandt, confirmed Rascher's belief that Poles and Russians were beyond the pale and should be given no amnesty of any kind.

FREEZING EXPERIMENTS

The deep interest of the German Air Force in capitalizing on the availability of inmates of concentration camps for experimental purposes is even more apparent in the case of the freezing experiments. These, too, were conducted at Dachau. They began immediately after the high-altitude experiments were completed and they continued until the spring of 1943...

The purpose of these experiments was to determine the most effective way of rewarming German aviators who were forced to parachute into the North Sea. The evidence will show that in the course of these experiments, the victims were forced to remain outdoors without clothing in freezing weather from nine to 14 hours. In other cases, they were forced to remain in a tank of iced water for three hours at a time. The water experiments are described in a report by Rascher written in August 1942. I quote:

"Electrical measurements gave low temperature readings of 26.4° in the stomach and 26.5° in the rectum. Fatalities occurred only when the brain stem and the back of the head were also chilled. Autopsies of such fatal cases always revealed large amounts of free blood, up to 1/2 liter, in the cranial cavity. The heart invariably showed extreme dilation of the right chamber. As soon as the temperature in those experiments reached 28°, the experimental subjects died invariably, despite all attempts at resuscitation."

Other documents set forth that from time to time the temperature of the water would be lowered by 10° Centigrade and a quart of blood would be taken from an artery in the subject's throat for analysis. The organs of the victims who died were extracted and sent to the Pathological Institute at Munich.

Rewarming of the subjects was attempted by various means, most commonly and successfully in a very hot bath. Himmler personally ordered that rewarming by the warmth of human bodies also be attempted, and the inhuman villains who conducted these experiments promptly produced four Gypsy women from the Ravensbrueck concentration camp. When the women had arrived, rewarming was attempted by placing the chilled victim between two naked women...

MALARIA EXPERIMENTS

Another series of experiments carried out at the Dachau concentration camp concerned immunization for and treatment of malaria. Over 1,200 inmates of practically every nationality were experimented upon. Many persons who participated in these experiments have already been tried before a general military court held at Dachau, and the findings of that court will be laid before this Tribunal. The malaria experiments were carried out under the general supervision of Dr. Schilling, with whom the defendant Sievers and others in the box collaborated. The evidence will show that healthy persons were infected by mosquitoes or by injections from the glands of mosquitoes. Catholic priests were among the subjects. The defendant Gebhardt kept Himmler informed of the progress of these experiments. Rose furnished Schilling with fly eggs for them, and others of the defendants participated in various ways which the evidence will demonstrate.

After the victims had been infected, they were variously treated with quinine, neosalvarsan, pyramidon, antipyrin, and several combinations of these drugs. Many deaths occurred from excessive doses of neosalvarsan and pyramidon. According to the findings of the Dachau court, malaria was the direct cause of 30 deaths and 300 to 400 others died as the result of subsequent complications.

MUSTARD GAS EXPERIMENTS

The experiments concerning mustard gas were conducted at Sachsenhausen, Natzweiler, and other concentration camps and extended over the entire period of the war. Wounds were deliberately inflicted on the victims, and the wounds were then infected with mustard gas. Other subjects were forced to inhale the gas, or to take it internally in liquid form, and still others were injected with the gas. A report on these experiments written at the end of 1939 described certain cases in which wounds were inflicted on both arms of the human guinea pigs and then infected, and the report states: "The arms in most of the cases are badly swollen and pains are enormous."

The alleged purpose of these experiments was to discover an effective treatment for the burns caused by mustard gas. In 1944

15

the experiments were coordinated with a general program for research into gas warfare. A decree issued by Hitler in March 1944 ordered the defendant Karl Brandt to push medical research in connection with gas warfare...

RAVENSBRUECK EXPERIMENTS CONCERNING SULFANILAMIDE AND OTHER DRUGS; BONE, MUSCLE, AND NERVE REGENERATION AND BONE TRANSPLANTATION

The experiments conducted principally on the female inmates of Ravensbrueck concentration camp were perhaps the most barbaric of all. These concerned bone, muscle, and nerve regeneration and bone transplantation, and experiments with sulfanilamide and other drugs. They were carried out by the defendants Fischer and Oberheuser under the direction of the defendant Gebhardt.

In one set of experiments, incisions were made on the legs of several of the camp inmates for the purpose of simulating battle-caused infections. A bacterial culture, or fragments of wood shavings, or tiny pieces of glass were forced into the wound. After several days, the wounds were treated with sulfanilamide. Grawitz, the head of the SS Medical Service, visited Ravensbrueck and received a report on these experiments directly from the defendant Fischer. Grawitz thereupon directed that the wounds inflicted on the subjects should be even more severe so that conditions similar to those prevailing at the front lines would be more completely simulated.

Bullet wounds were simulated on the subjects by tying off the blood vessels at both ends of the incision. A gangrene-producing culture was then placed in the wounds. Severe infection resulted within 24 hours. Operations were then performed on the infected areas, and the wounds were treated with sulfanilamide. In each of the many sulfanilamide experiments, some of the subjects were wounded and infected but were not given sulfanilamide, so as to compare their reactions with those who received treatment...

SEA-WATER EXPERIMENTS

For the sea-water experiments we return to Dachau. They were conducted in 1944 at the behest of the German Air Force and the German Navy in order to develop a method of rendering sea water drinkable. Meetings to discuss this problem were held in

May 1944, attended by representatives of the Luftwaffe, the Navy, and I.G. Farben. The defendants Becker-Freyseng and Schaefer were among the participants. It was agreed to conduct a series of experiments in which the subjects, fed only with shipwreck emergency rations, would be divided into four groups. One group would receive no water at all; the second would drink ordinary sea water; the third would drink sea water processed by the so-called "Berka" method, which concealed the taste but did not alter the saline content; the fourth would drink sea water treated so as to remove the salt.

Since it was expected that the subjects would die, or at least suffer severe impairment of health, it was decided at the meeting in May 1944 that only persons furnished by Himmler could be used...The tests were actually begun in July 1944. The defendant Beiglboeck supervised the experiments, in the course of which the Gypsy subjects underwent terrible suffering, became delirious or developed convulsions, and some died.

EPIDEMIC JAUNDICE

The epidemic jaundice experiments, which took place at Sachsenhausen and Natzweiler concentration camps, were instigated by the defendant Karl Brandt. A letter written in 1943 by Grawitz stresses the enormous military importance of developing an inoculation against epidemic jaundice, which had spread extensively in the Waffen SS and the German Army, particularly in southern Russia. In some companies, up to 60 percent casualties from epidemic jaundice had occurred...Other evidence will indicate that the scope of these experiments was subsequently enlarged and that murder, torture, and death resulted from them.

STERILIZATION EXPERIMENTS

In the sterilization experiments conducted by the defendants at Auschwitz, Ravensbrueck, and other concentration camps, the destructive nature of the Nazi medical program comes out most forcibly. The Nazis were searching for methods of extermination, both by murder and sterilization, of large population groups, by the most scientific and least conspicuous means. They were developing a new branch of medical science which would give them the scientific tools for the planning and practice of genocide. The primary purpose was to discover an inexpensive, unobtrusive, and rapid method of sterilization which could be used to wipe out

Russians, Poles, Jews, and other people. Surgical sterilization was thought to be too slow and expensive to be used on a mass scale. A method to bring about an unnoticed sterilization was thought desirable.

Medicinal sterilizations were therefore carried out. Dr. Madaus had stated that *caladium seguinum,* a drug obtained from a North American plant, if taken orally or by injection, would bring about sterilization. In 1941 the defendant Pokorny called this to Himmler's attention, and suggested that it should be developed and used against Russian prisoners of war. I quote one paragraph from Pokorny's letter written at that time:

"If, on the basis of this research, it were possible to produce a drug which after a relatively short time, effects an imperceptible sterilization on human beings, then we would have a powerful new weapon at our disposal. The thought alone that the three million Bolsheviks, who are at present German prisoners, could be sterilized so that they could be used as laborers but be prevented from reproduction, opens the most far-reaching perspectives."

As a result of Pokorny's suggestion, experiments were conducted on concentration camp inmates to test the effectiveness of the drug. At the same time efforts were made to grow the plant on a large scale in hothouses.

At the Auschwitz concentration camp sterilization experiments were also conducted on a large scale by Dr. Karl Clauberg, who had developed a method of sterilizing women based on the injection of an irritating solution. Several thousand Jews and Gypsies were sterilized at Auschwitz by this method.

Conversely, surgical operations were performed on sexually abnormal inmates at Buchenwald in order to determine whether their virility could be increased by the transplantation of glands. Out of 14 subjects of these experiments, at least two died. The defendant Gebhardt also personally conducted sterilizations at Ravensbrueck by surgical operation...

TYPHUS (FLECKFIEBER) AND RELATED EXPERIMENTS

From December 1941, until near the end of the war, a large program of medical experimentation was carried out upon concentration camp inmates at Buchenwald and Natzweiler to investigate the value of various vaccines. This research involved a variety of diseases — typhus, yellow fever, smallpox, paratyphoid A and B, cholera, and diphtheria. A dozen or more of the defendants were involved in these experiments which were characterized by the most cynical disregard of human life. Hundreds of persons died. The experiments concerning typhus – known in Germany as *Fleckfieber* or "spot fever," but not to be confused with American spotted fever – were particularly appalling...

The general pattern of these typhus experiments was as follows. A group of concentration camp inmates, selected from the healthier ones who had some resistance to disease, were injected with an anti-typhus vaccine, the efficacy of which was to be tested. Thereafter, all the persons in the group would be infected with typhus. At the same time, other inmates who had not been vaccinated were also infected for purposes of comparison – these unvaccinated victims were called the "control" group. But perhaps the most wicked and murderous circumstance in this whole case is that still other inmates were deliberately infected with typhus with the sole purpose of keeping the typhus virus alive and generally available in the blood stream of the inmates...

POISON EXPERIMENTS

Here again the defendants were studying how to kill, and the scene is Buchenwald. Poisons were administered to Russian prisoners of war in their food, and German doctors stood behind a curtain to watch the reactions of the prisoners. Some of the Russians died immediately, and the survivors were killed in order to permit autopsies...

INCENDIARY BOMB EXPERIMENTS

These experiments were likewise carried out at Buchenwald, and the Ding diary gives us the facts. In November 1943 five persons were deliberately burned with phosphorous material taken from an English incendiary bomb. The victims were permanently and seriously injured...

ABUSE OF SCIENCE, POWER

The 20 physicians in the dock range from leaders of German scientific medicine, with excellent international reputations, down to the dregs of the German medical profession. All of them have

19

in common a callous lack of consideration and human regard for, and an unprincipled willingness to abuse their power over the poor, unfortunate, defenseless creatures who had been deprived of their rights by a ruthless and criminal government. All of them violated the Hippocratic commandments which they had solemnly sworn to uphold and abide by, including the fundamental principles never to do harm – *primum non nocere...*

NO OPTIONS, NO CONSENT

None of the victims of the atrocities perpetrated by these defendants were volunteers, and this is true regardless of what these unfortunate people may have said or signed before their tortures began. Most of the victims had not been condemned to death, and those who had been were not criminals, unless it be a crime to be a Jew, or a Pole, or a Gypsy, or a Russian prisoner of war.

Whatever book or treatise on medical ethics we may examine, and whatever expert on forensic medicine we may question, will say that it is a fundamental and inescapable obligation of every physician under any known system of law not to perform a dangerous experiment without the subject's consent...

CRIMINAL AND SCIENTIFIC FAILURES

These experiments revealed nothing which civilized medicine can use. It was, indeed, ascertained that phenol or gasoline injected intravenously will kill a man inexpensively and within 60 seconds. This and a few other "advances" are all in the field of thanatology. There is no doubt that a number of these new methods may be useful to criminals everywhere, and there is no doubt that they may be useful to a criminal state. Certain advance in destructive methodology we cannot deny, and indeed from Himmler's standpoint this may well have been the principal objective. Apart from these deadly fruits, the experiments were not only criminal but a scientific failure.

READING

2

THE NUREMBERG CODE

LeRoy Walters, Ph.D.

LeRoy Walters is the Joseph P. Kennedy, Senior Professor of Christian Ethics at the Kennedy Institute of Ethics and Professor of Philosophy at Georgetown University, Washington, D.C.

■ **POINTS TO CONSIDER**

1. Define the Nuremberg Code.

2. What events shaped the principles of the code?

3. Describe actions taken by the World Medical Association.

Excerpted from the testimony of LeRoy Walters before the Subcommittee on Energy and Power of the House of Representatives Committee on Energy and Commerce, January 18, 1994.

In August 1947 a detailed code of research ethics was presented as part of the judgment in the Nuremberg medical trial. The ten principles of the Nuremberg Code covered the topics of voluntary consent, research design, prior animal experimentation, limits on anticipated harm to research subjects, the qualifications of investigators, and the freedom of subjects to withdraw from a study at any time.

THE NUREMBERG CODE

Although the ten principles of the Nuremberg Code have been frequently quoted, it is important in this context to recall the precise content of research ethics in August of 1947.

1. The voluntary consent of the human subject is absolutely essential...

2. The experiment should be such as to yield fruitful results for the good of society, unprocurable by other methods or means of study, and not random or unnecessary in nature.

3. The experiment should be so designed and based on the results of animal experimentation and a knowledge of the natural history of the disease or other problem under study that the anticipated results will justify the performance of the experiment.

4. The experiment should be so conducted as to avoid all unnecessary physical and mental suffering and injury.

5. No experiment should be conducted where there is an *a priori* reason to believe that death or disabling injury will occur; except, perhaps in those experiments where the experimental physicians also serve as subjects.

6. The degree of risk to be taken should never exceed that determined by the humanitarian importance of the problem to be solved by the experiment.

7. Proper preparations should be made and adequate facilities provided to protect the experimental subject against even remote possibilities of injury, disability or death.

8. The experiment should be conducted only by scientifically

qualified persons. The highest degree of skill and care should be required through all stages of the experiment of those who conduct or engage in the experiment.

9. During the course of the experiment, the human subject should be at liberty to bring the experiment to an end if he has reached the physical or mental state where continuation of the experiment seems to him to be impossible.

10. During the course of the experiment the scientist in charge must be prepared to terminate the experiment at any stage, if he has probable cause to believe, in the exercise of the good faith, superior skill and careful judgment required of him that a continuation of the experiment is likely to result in injury, disability, or death to the experimental subject

[Trials of War Criminals Before the Nuremberg Military Tribunals Under Control Council Law No. 10 (Washington, D.C.: U.S. Government Printing Office, 1950), II, 181-182].

In August 1947 a detailed code of research ethics was presented as part of the judgment in the Nuremberg medical trial. The ten principles of the Nuremberg Code covered the topics of voluntary consent, research design, prior animal experimentation, limits on anticipated harm to research subjects, the qualifications of investigators, and the freedom of subjects to withdraw from a study at any time.

Representatives to the United Nations Commission on Human Rights were deeply concerned about the Nazi medical experiments and asserted a general human right not to be a subject of medical or scientific experimentation "against one's will" (1948) or "without one's free consent" (1952 and 1958).

WORLD MEDICAL ASSOCIATION

At the second annual meeting of the World Medical Association, held in Geneva, the General Assembly adopted a detailed statement entitled "War Crimes and Medicine: The German Betrayal and a Restatement of the Ethics of Medicine." The statement drew heavily on the evidence compiled in *German Medical War Crimes: A Summary of Information*. While the statement notes that "experiments without consent" were performed on human subjects, the primary focus of the statement is on condemning the harms inflicted on subjects, approving the

MORAL DECLINE OF THE ELITE

Scientific skill is no inoculant against moral collapse; indeed, if scientific skill has any relation to moral decline, history suggests that it may be a risk factor. Clearly, Leo Alexander believed that it was no accident that medicine's worst corruption had occurred among its best technicians.

Patrick G. Derr, "Hadamar, Hippocrates, and the Future of Medicine: Reflections on Euthanasia and the History of German Medicine," **Issues in Law and Medicine**, vol. 4, no. 4, 1989:491.

Nuremberg judgments, and urging the German medical profession to acknowledge its collaboration in evil. In conclusion, the statement urges that all new physicians take an oath that embodies the spirit of the ancient Hippocratic Oath. This updated oath, now called "The Declaration of Geneva," included the following two points:

• I will not permit considerations of religion, nationality, race, party politics or social standing to intervene between my duty and my patient.

• I will maintain the utmost respect for human life, from the time of conception; even under threat, I will not use my medical knowledge contrary to the laws of humanity [*World Medical Bulletin 1(1): 15, April 1949*].

In October 1948, the World Medical Association condemned the Nazi medical experiments and urged physicians to act with the utmost respect for human life and never to use their medical knowledge contrary to the laws of humanity. By early 1949, the book *Doctors of Infamy* made the Nazi medical war crimes and the ten principles of the Nuremberg Code readily accessible to any person who had not previously been aware of the crimes, the trial, and the code.

MEDICAL ETHICS

Psychiatrist Leo Alexander published an article entitled "Medical Science under Dictatorship" in the *New England Journal of Medicine* [241(2): 39-47; July 14, 1949]. The primary subjects of the article were the Nazi euthanasia program, the science of

ANATOMY OF THE MURDERED?

Every day before they go into surgery, doctors around the world consult their Pernkopf anatomical atlas...David Williams, professor and director of medical illustration at Purdue University, calls Pernkopf's seven-volume "Topographische Anatomie des Menschen" ("Topographical Anatomy of Man") "the standard by which all other illustrated anatomical works are measured."

"They're masterpieces," Williams said. "Monumental."

But 50 years after their initial publication, the Pernkopf illustrations have come under fire, igniting debate in the medical community. Many people now believe that Eduard Pernkopf, the Austrian anatomist for whom the atlas is named, and his team of artists used specimens taken from victims of Nazi concentration camps for their illustrations.

Carol Schoettler, "A Medical Book with Nazi Origins," **Baltimore Sun**, August, 1997.

annihilation, and "medicomilitary research," for example, the freezing experiments. After commending Dutch physicians for their resistance to Nazi efforts to secure their collaboration in identifying patients who could not be rehabilitated, Alexander noted that U.S. medicine was showing early signs of intolerance for the chronically ill. Alexander warned against a medical ethic that says, "What is useful is right," and urged a return to "the older premises, which were the emotional foundation and driving force for an amazingly successful quest to increase powers of healing." There was no mention in the article of the Nuremberg Code.

The four Geneva Conventions of August 12, 1949, clearly reflected the concerns expressed in the Nuremberg Code. The First and Second Conventions specified in Article 12 that members of the armed forces shall "not be subjected to biological experiments." The Third Convention provided that "no prisoner of war may be subjected to physical mutilation or to medical or scientific experiments of any kind which are not justified by the medical, dental, or hospital treatment of the prisoner concerned and carried out in his interest." Article 32 of the Fourth

Convention (protecting civilian persons in times of war) prohibited medical or scientific experiments not necessitated by the medical treatment of the protected person (Perley, et al., "The Nuremberg Code," pp. 153-154).

In 1949, the framers of the Geneva Conventions also wished to avoid a repetition of the Nazi medical war crimes and, therefore, incorporated explicit protections against unwanted biological or medical experimentation into all four new conventions.

THE ROAD TO GENOCIDE

James A. Maccaro

James A. Maccaro practices law on Long Island, New York. He has written "Medical Science Under Dictatorship," which has been reprinted as a 32-page pamphlet that can be obtained for $2.00 (which includes postage and handling) from Bibliographic Press, P.O. Box 5433, Flushing, NY 11354.

■ POINTS TO CONSIDER

1. Describe the shift that occurred in medical attitudes in the 1930s.

2. According to the author, what was the scale and scope of euthanasia in Germany before the war, and who controlled policy oversight?

3. Discuss the significance of the "Life Not Worth Living Philosophy."

4. Contrast the actions of the Dutch physicians with those of the Germans.

James A. Maccaro, "'From Small Beginnings': The Road to Genocide," **The Freeman**, August 1997: 497-81. © 1997 Foundation for Economic Freedom, Inc. Reprinted with permission.

The German medical profession fully cooperated with the Nazis and, indeed, was responsible for some of the most disturbing outrages of the Nazi regime.

Dr. Leo Alexander, a prominent American psychiatrist, was the chief U.S. medical consultant at the Nuremberg War Crimes Trials that judged Nazi leaders following World War II. One question in particular perplexed him: Why was the German medical profession unable to effectively resist the Nazis?

As he searched in German archives, Dr. Alexander was puzzled by the lack of documentation of resistance by doctors. He assumed that German physicians, as scientists devoted to relieving human suffering, were appalled by the Nazis. He knew of the high regard the German public had for doctors, who were typically among the leading citizens of their communities, and expected to find many examples of doctors who used their prestige to resist the Nazis. Yet he found no such evidence. In shocking contrast, Dr. Alexander discovered that the German medical profession fully cooperated with the Nazis and, indeed, was responsible for some of the most disturbing outrages of the Nazi regime.

TOTAL COOPERATION

Dr. Alexander was forced by the facts to change the focus of his research to an examination of the process by which the German medical profession came under the total domination of Hitler's government. He set forth his findings in the July 14, 1949, issue of *The New England Journal of Medicine*. In this remarkable study, "Medical Science Under Dictatorship," Dr. Alexander described how the German medical profession, in the words of Malcolm Muggeridge, "sleepwalked to the collectivist-authoritarian way of life."

Dr. Alexander discovered that the Nazi Holocaust began with "a subtle shift...in attitude" that accepted a philosophy of government that judged people based upon their perceived costs and benefits to the state. The first manifestation of this was the open discussion during the time of the Weimar republic, prior to Hitler's takeover of Germany, of government schemes for the sterilization and euthanasia of people with severe psychiatric illnesses. By 1936, medical extermination was widely and openly practiced, and the category of those deemed to be a burden to the state and therefore socially unfit to live had expanded to encompass all people with chronic illness.

29

DEATHS AS STATE POLICY

On September 1, 1939, euthanasia was officially recognized as state policy, and two government agencies were established to carry out the killings in an efficient manner. They were cynically named the "Reich's Work Committee of Institutions for Cure and Care," which dealt with adults, and the "Reich's Committee for Scientific Approach to Severe Illness Due to Heredity and Constitution," for children. Separate organizations were created to transport patients to killing centers and to collect the cost of the killing from the next of kin, who were told that the victim had died of natural causes.

Doctors were required to report on all patients who had been sick for five years or more or who were medically unable to work and unlikely to recover. The decision about whether someone should be put to death was generally made by psychiatrists who taught at leading universities. These "consultants" never examined or even saw the patient and based their decisions on brief questionnaires, which contained information about race, ethnic origin, marital status, next of kin, financial resources, and whether and by whom the patient was visited.

MERCY KILLING TO EXTERMINATION

What began as a slow acceptance of "mercy killings" in rare cases of extreme mental illness soon expanded to mass extermination on an unprecedented scale. Among those killed were people with epilepsy, infantile paralysis, Parkinson's disease, depression, multiple sclerosis, and various infirmities of old age. In short, all people who were unable to work and not considered rehabilitable were killed. One physician later admitted:

The victims were selected from the various wards of the institutions according to an excessively simple and quick method. Most institutions did not have enough physicians, and what physicians existed were either too busy or did not care, and they delegated the selection to the nurses and attendants. Whoever looked sick or was otherwise a problem was put on a list and was transported to the killing center. The worst thing about this business was it produced a certain brutalization of the nursing personnel. They got to simply pick out those whom they did not like, and the doctors had so many patients that they did not even know them, and put their names on the list.

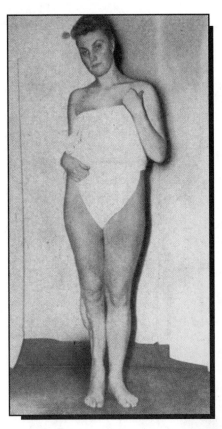

DOCUMENT NO-1080 E

PROSECUTION
EXHIBIT 219E

Exposures of the witness
Maria Kusmierczuk who
underwent sulfanilamide
and bone experiments
while an inmate of
the Ravensbrueck
concentration camp.

DOCUMENT NO-1080 F

PROSECUTION
EXHIBIT 219F

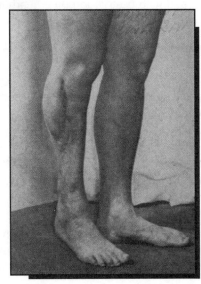

Source: "Doctors' Trial," **Germany
Military Tribunals, Trials of War
Criminals:** Vol. I: 27-74. Dec. 9,
1946-July 18, 1947

It is estimated that 275,000 Germans were exterminated in the killing centers; this provided extensive opportunities to perfect the methods that were later used in the concentration camps. The next step taken by the German medical profession was the accumulation and use of human material obtained from the exterminated for medical research. For instance, one physician obtained 500 brains for use in his neurological research. This was soon followed by the use of live people for "terminal human experiments," a practice that was openly accepted by the German medical profession.

"A LIFE NOT WORTHY TO BE LIVED"

Dr. Alexander demonstrated in *Medical Science Under Dictatorship* that by the early 1940s, the German medical profession had become fully implicated with the Nazi regime and its death camps. Moreover, he outlined how this monstrous outcome originated "from small beginnings." It started with acceptance of the "progressive" and "rational" idea that some people had "a life not worthy to be lived" and were a burden to society and to the state. Once this idea was acted upon, and physicians became accustomed to it, the extermination system expanded to include all people considered for any reason to be a financial burden to the state, followed by all those considered to be disloyal or a threat to the government and, ultimately, anyone considered undesirable by the government. Once the first German mental patient was put to death, a chain of events was begun that only ended with destruction on a nearly unfathomable scale, including the murder of the majority of European Jews.

THE DUTCH EXAMPLE

Dr. Alexander contrasted the actions of the German medical profession with those of doctors in the Netherlands under German occupation, who refused to take the first small step to genocide. In December 1944, an order was issued by the Nazi authorities to all Dutch physicians: "It is the duty of the doctor, through advice and effort, conscientiously and to his best ability, to assist as helper to person entrusted to his care in the maintenance, improvement and re-establishment of his vitality, physical efficiency and health. The accomplishment of this duty is a public task."

This statement might appear on first reading to be unobjectionable and innocuous. However, the Dutch medical profession, which was aware of the extermination system in place on the

SCANDINAVIAN SCANDALS

According to the Swedish newspaper *Dagens Nyheter*, Maria Nordin was one of 60,000 Swedes, 6,000 Danes and 40,000 Norwegians sterilized under explicit eugenics policies that began in the Nordic countries before Hitler came to power in Germany and didn't end until 1976.

Nurtured by social democrats but reminiscent of national socialism, the policies resulted in the sterilization of more than 100,000 Swedes, Danes and Norwegians whose race, lifestyle or mental capacities were deemed undesirable. Ninety percent of them were women...

"Sweden Soul-Searching after Revelations About Sterilizations," **Scripts Howard News Service**, August, 1997.

other side of the Dutch-German border, recognized that this order would serve as a basis for the promulgation of a new standard of care that would place first priority upon the return of patients to productivity for the state, rather than the relief of suffering. Physicians would consequently be subordinated to the state and its interest to maximize "utility."

Dutch physicians unanimously refused to comply. When the Nazis threatened to revoke uncooperating doctors' licenses to practice, all doctors returned their licenses and closed their offices, but continued to see patients in private. The Nazis then arrested 100 Dutch doctors and sent them to concentration camps, but the medical profession refused to back down. The result was that no Dutch doctor participated in a killing, and the Nazi plans for medical exterminations in the Netherlands were not carried out.

Dr. Alexander concluded:

It is obvious that if the medical profession of a small nation under the conqueror's heel could resist so effectively, the German medical profession could likewise have resisted had they not taken the fatal first step. It is the first seemingly innocent step away from principle that frequently decides a life of crime. Corrosion begins in microscopic proportions.

4

THE JAPANESE ANALOGUE

Michael A. Grodin

Michael A. Grodin reviewed the book Factories of Death *for the* Hastings Center Report. *He coedited the book* Nazi Doctors and the Nuremberg Code *(Oxford: 1992). The Hastings Center carries out educational research programs on ethical issues.*

■ POINTS TO CONSIDER

1. What parallels does Grodin draw between Nazi and Japanese medical experiments?

2. Summarize the nature of the experiments the book contends occurred in Japanese camps.

3. Contrast the fate of the Nazi and Japanese doctors after the war.

4. Evaluate the reviewer's belief about the "medicalization" of military/political ideology.

Michael A. Grodin, "The Japanese Analogue," **Hastings Center Report,** September/October 1996: 37-8. Reproduced by permission. © 1996, The Hastings Center.

Medicalization of military and political ideology leads to an objectification of humans as means to an end.

The wrongs which we seek to condemn and punish have been so calculated, so malignant, and so devastating, that civilization cannot tolerate their being ignored because it cannot survive their being repeated.

This is a quotation from the prosecution's opening statement at the Nuremberg doctors' trial of 9 December 1946. That public trial revealed the widescale horrors of Nazi physicians' involvement in human experimentation, torture, and murder of concentration camp prisoners. The Japanese Kwantung Army physicians conducted identical human experimentation, torture, and murder of prisoners in Manchuria and China proper between 1932 and 1945, but no similar trial exposed their crimes against humanity.

JAPAN'S SECRET

Several texts in English and Japanese have focused on Japan's secret biological weapon research program during World War II, beginning with the first report on "Japan's Biological Weapon 1930-1945" in the *Bulletin of the Atomic Scientists*. But, until recently, there has been no complete account of this period. Meticulous records of the Japanese Army were uncovered in China as well as in Russia and Japan. The documents and the testimony of senior Japanese officers and data stored in the United States at Fort Detrick in Maryland form the substance of the comprehensive and important text, *Factories of Death: Japanese Biological Warfare 1932-1945 and the American Cover-Up*, written by Sheldon H. Harris, professor emeritus of history, California State University at Northridge.

The first part of this book focuses on so-called Unit 731 and the prisoner camps at Ping Fan, Beiyinhe, Changchun, and Nanking in Manchuria and China. In 1932 the Japanese army sent Major Ishii Shiro (who later rose to lieutenant general), a physician and immunologist in the medical corps, to Harbin in newly conquered Manchuria to set up a biological warfare facility. Thus began over a decade of both offensive and defensive biological warfare research.

The Japanese physicians, reinforced by their racial hygienist and eugenic views of racial superiority, saw their human subjects as experimental "material." The Nazi doctors had referred to the

JAPANESE BIOLOGICAL WEAPON

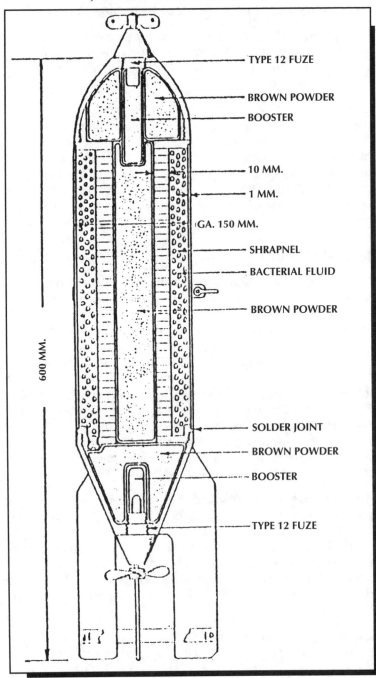

TYPE 12 FUZE

BROWN POWDER

BOOSTER

10 MM.

1 MM.

GA. 150 MM.

SHRAPNEL

BACTERIAL FLUID

BROWN POWDER

SOLDER JOINT

BROWN POWDER

BOOSTER

TYPE 12 FUZE

600 MM.

Source: U.S. Army Report on Japanese Biological Warfare Activities, May 31, 1946.

Jewish, Gypsy, and Polish subjects of their research as "Untermenschen" (subhumans). The Japanese physicians referred to their human "guinea pigs," as "Manchurian monkeys" and "maruta" (logs of wood). These "logs" were the "products" of the central prisoner camp at Ping Fan, which was referred to as a "lumber mill." The experimental subjects used by the Japanese included Han Chinese, White Russians, Soviet prisoners captured in border skirmishes, Mongolian and Korean political prisoners, and the mentally handicapped. Harris makes a convincing case that U.S. prisoners of war probably were not used as subjects.

THE EXPERIMENTS

Three types of experiments were conducted at the "factories of death." Laboratory experiments on individual subjects were conducted at Ping Fan and other units. Open air experiments were conducted to test the effectiveness of a prototype biological warfare delivery system. Further field tests exposed civilian and military personnel to biological pathogens. Japanese physicians conducted experiments with plague, cholera, typhoid, dysentery, anthrax, tetanus, gas gangrene, tuberculosis, and other viruses and rickettsia. Their research "successes" earned Dr. Ishii and his colleagues more money from the Japanese war ministry. By the mid-1930s more facilities were established and four stations were set up for the production of biological warfare materials.

How were experiments conducted? Both adults and children were fed and injected with biological organisms and then closely monitored. Bulletin boards in the Ping Fan laboratory recorded the dates, number of "logs," number of injections, and the number of "hearts" or "livers" used. Subjects were dissected, often while the person was still conscious, in order to monitor the course of disease until death. Such actions directly parallel the ghastly work of Dr. Mengele in the Nazi death camps. As in the Nazi experiments, Japanese physicians injected subjects with potassium cyanide, jolted prisoners with electric shocks, and exposed subjects to phosphene gas. Both Nazi and Japanese physicians conducted high altitude experiments and freezing experiments. Chinese prisoners' extremities were frozen to test methods of rewarming.

Harris estimates that 12,000 prisoners died as a direct result of medical experimentation, and field tests accounted for another 200,000 to 250,000 deaths. Deaths attributable to Nazi experiments have been estimated at 100,000 deaths.

BRAIN RESEARCH

The Togo Unit employed gruesome tactics to secure specimens of select body organs. If Ishii or one of his co-workers wished to do research on the human brain, then they would order the guards to find them a useful sample. A prisoner would be taken from his cell. Guards would hold him while another guard would smash the victim's head open with an ax. His brain would be extracted and rushed immediately to the laboratory. The body would then be whisked off to the pathologist, and then to the crematorium for the usual disposal.

Sheldon H. Harris, **Factories of Death: Japanese Biological Warfare, 1932-45, and the American Cover-Up**, New York: Rutledge, 1994, 28.

COVER-UP

The second half of the book focuses on the postwar cover-up by U.S. scientists and soldiers. The negotiations that led to exempting these Japanese physicians from prosecution as war criminals in exchange for the data from their experiments is as disturbing as the research itself.

No Japanese physicians were brought to justice at the 1948 Tokyo war crimes trial. Ishii and the other physicians were given immunity for sharing what they knew with U.S. intelligence. This despite the fact that the same medical experiments were condemned by the 1947 Nuremberg doctors' trial, which was conducted under U.S. auspices and under U.S. law. But at the outset of the cold war, the U.S. Army Chemical Warfare Service Special Projects Division on Biological Warfare at Fort Detrick believed that the "intelligence value" of the data from Unit 731 was more important than prosecuting war crimes and crimes against humanity.

After the war Ishii and his physician colleagues continued to flourish in the Japanese medical establishment. Several went on to such prestigious positions as directors of the Japanese National Institutes of Health and National Cancer Institute, president of the Japanese Medical Association, dean of a Japanese medical school, a Japanese university president, and Japan's surgeon general.

THE OLD FARMER

He is a cheerful old farmer who jokes as he serves rice cakes made by his wife and then he switches easily to explaining what it is like to cut open a 30-year-old man who is tied naked to a bed and dissect him alive, without anesthetic.

"The fellow knew that it was over for him and so he didn't struggle when they led him into the room and tied him down," recalled the 72-year-old farmer, then a medical assistant in a Japanese army unit in China in World War II. "But when I picked up the scalpel, that's when he began screaming. I cut him open from the chest to the stomach and he screamed terribly and his face was all twisted in agony. He made this unimaginable sound, he was screaming so horribly. But then finally he stopped. This was all in a day's work for the surgeons, but it really left an impression on me because it was my first time"...

Nicholas D. Kristof, "Unlocking a Deadly Secret," **Star Tribune**, March 18, 1995. © **New York Times**.

POISONED LEGACY

And the story is not over. In 1995 the Japanese government sent military and chemical experts back to China to seal poison vats discovered by the Chinese. It is estimated that the Japanese abandoned over two million decaying shells and one hundred tons of toxins.

What can we learn from this incredible story? Medicalization of military and political ideology leads to an objectification of humans as means to an end. Even the U.S. military has borrowed the rationalizations used by Nazi and Japanese war criminals. When confronted with revelations about its World War II experiments on servicemen who were subjected to poison gas, mustard gas, chemical agents, and radiation, its justification, like that of the Nazis and Japanese, has been that the experiments were done "for the country" and for "the good of society."

We must continue to study these cases because we "cannot survive their being repeated." In the words of the chief prosecutor at the Nuremberg doctors' trial:

ALLIED PRISONERS

"They were brutal to each other, but they also were killing and starving innocent, helpless people – and that's beyond any human instinct I know of," Schwarz says. "They were indoctrinated to believe we were racially inferior, and they were constantly telling us that, because we allowed ourselves to be captured, we had no soul"...

"They were beaten until they bled, then beaten for bleeding, denied medical treatment and starved, then worked to death as slave labor," says Daws, who interviewed and cross-checked the stories of hundreds of former POWs. Prisoners were tortured, mutilated and beheaded. At one women's camp, pregnant prisoners on the verge of labor had their ankles tightly bound with chains, then were tossed aside to die in agony.

Japan decreed death for "talking without permission, showing individualism or raising loud voices." In Germany's World War II prison camps, about one percent of the American prisoners died in captivity. But in Japanese camps, the killing was accelerating at such a rate that, had the war lasted another year, there would not have been a single POW left alive, says Daws.

David Wood, "Memories of Japanese Camps," **Newhouse News Series**, April, 1995.

It is our deep obligation to all peoples of the world to show why and how these things happened. It is incumbent upon us to set forth with conspicuous clarity the ideas and motives which moved these defendants to treat their fellow men as less than beasts. The perverse thoughts and distorted concepts which brought about these savageries are not dead. They cannot be killed by force of arms. They must not become a spreading cancer in the breast of humanity. They must be cut out and exposed... *Factories of Death* exposes the "cancer" among the Japanese physicians. It reminds us that even physicians dedicated to health and healing can turn to torture and murder in the service of country and ideology. Wherever war, politics, or ideology serve to objectify humans as mere subjects, we all lose our humanity.

WHAT IS POLITICAL BIAS?

This activity may be used as an individualized study guide for students in libraries and resource centers or as a discussion catalyst in small group and classroom discussions.

Many readers are unaware that written material usually expresses an opinion or bias. The skill to read with insight and understanding requires the ability to detect different kinds of bias. Political bias, race bias, sex bias, ethnocentric bias and religious bias are five basic kinds of opinions expressed in editorials and literature that attempt to persuade. This activity will focus on political bias defined in the glossary below.

Five Kinds of Editorial Opinion or Bias

Sex Bias — The expression of dislike for and/or feeling of superiority over a person because of gender or sexual preference.

Race Bias — The expression of dislike for and/or feeling of superiority over a racial group.

Ethnocentric Bias — The expression of a belief that one's own group, race, religion, culture, or nation is superior. Ethnocentric persons judge others by their own standards and values.

Political Bias — The expression of political opinions and attitudes about government-related issues on the local, state, national or international level.

Religious Bias — The expression of a religious belief or attitude.

Guidelines

Read through the following statements and decide which ones represent political opinion or bias. Evaluate each statement by using the method indicated below.

- **Mark (P)** *for statements that reflect any political opinion or bias.*
- **Mark (F)** *for any factual statements.*
- **Mark (O)** *for statements of opinion.*
- **Mark (N)** *for any statements that you are not sure about.*

_____ 1. Scientific skill is no inoculant against moral collapse; history suggests that it may be a risk factor.

_____ 2. The German medical profession fully cooperated with the Nazis and, indeed, was responsible for some of the most disturbing outrages of the Nazi regime.

_____ 3. By the early 1940s, the German medical profession had become fully implicated with the Nazi regime and its death camps.

_____ 4. The Japanese Kwantung Army physicians conducted human experimentation, torture, and murder of prisoners in Manchuria and China proper between 1932 and 1945, but no similar trial exposed their crimes against humanity.

_____ 5. Twelve thousand prisoners died as a direct result of medical experimentation, and field tests accounted for another 200,000 to 250,000 deaths. Deaths attributable to Nazi experiments have been estimated at 100,000 deaths.

_____ 6. No Japanese physicians were brought to justice at the 1948 Tokyo war crimes trial.

_____ 7. Foreign ideas have always been the biggest threat to American security.

_____ 8. The United Nations is our best hope for peace.

_____ 9. Religious persons who oppose saluting the flag should be monitored by the F.B.I.

_____10. The American economy has brought a superior way of life for the U.S. population.

_____11. The U.S. must have the most powerful military in the world to guarantee national security.

_____12. Jewish businessmen stick together and prevent others from fair competition.

CHAPTER 2

THE TUSKEGEE EXPERIMENT

CHRONOLOGY AND OVERVIEW

Centers for Disease Control

The Centers for Disease Control (CDC) is headquartered in Atlanta, Georgia. It is part of the U.S. Department of Health and Human Services. The CDC monitors and studies the health and disease patterns of the American people.

■ **POINTS TO CONSIDER**

1. When did the Tuskegee Syphilis Study begin?

2. How is the study defined?

3. Who filed a class action lawsuit, and how was it settled?

4. Describe the nature of the Belmont Report and also the Tuskegee Syphilis Study Legacy Committee.

Centers for Disease Control Chronology, 1996.

TUSKEGEE SYPHILIS STUDY: CHRONOLOGY AND OVERVIEW

1926 – Public Health Service (PHS) survey of incidence of syphilis begun in Macon County, Alabama, one of several sites in the United States.

1930 – Macon County Syphilis Control Demonstration Project begun. PHS received funding from the Rosenwald Fund. Treatment was a combination of neoarsphenamine and mercury. None of the 1400 patients received the full course of treatment.

1932 – Funding for the control demonstration project from Rosenwald Fund ended.

1932 – Tuskegee Syphilis Study began. This was a study of untreated syphilis in approximately 400 black men who were at least 25 years of age and had syphilis for five years or longer. Funded by the Public Health Service. Undertaken to compare the course of untreated syphilis in black men with the results of an Oslo study on untreated syphilis in whites. The study was supposed to last six to 12 months. Plan was to document course of disease and use that information to obtain funding for treatment. The Alabama Department of Health agreed to study with stipulation that some treatment be provided. Tuskegee Institute and local white physicians in Macon County also agreed to the study.

1933 – The Study continued past the original six to 12 months. It was decided to continue the study until the men died. Control group of 200+ men without syphilis added to the study.

1947 – Penicillin widely available for the treatment of syphilis.

1950 – Recommendation for the use of penicillin in late syphilis established. (Editor's note: During the study's lifetime, neither penicillin nor any other treatment was ever given to the 400 black men. These victims were used to study the course of syphilis in men.)

1957 – Responsibility for Study transferred to the Communicable Disease Center (now Centers for Disease Control and Prevention [CDC]).

1972 – News of the study reported in the *New York Times, Los Angeles Times,* and *Washington Star.* Tuskegee Syphilis Study *Ad Hoc* Panel composed by the Public Health Service to investigate the Study.

MEDICAL DECEPTION

In 1932, the United States Public Health Service (USPHS) initiated the Tuskegee Syphilis Study to document the natural history of syphilis. The subjects of the investigation were 399 poor black sharecroppers from Macon County, Alabama, with latent syphilis and 201 men without the disease who served as controls. The physicians conducting the Study deceived the men, telling them they were being treated for "bad blood." However, they deliberately denied treatment to the men with syphilis and went to extreme lengths to ensure that they would not receive any therapy from other sources. In exchange for their participation, the men received free meals, free medical examinations, and burial insurance. On 26 July, 1972, a front-page headline in the *New York Times* read, "Syphilis Victims in U.S. Study Went Untreated for 40 Years."

Tuskegee Syphilis Study Legacy Committee, May 20, 1996.

1972 – Study terminated by the Department of Health, Education, and Welfare (now the Department of Health and Human Services).

1973 – Public Health Service directed to provide necessary medical care. Men and their families contacted and given information about the study. Men and their families offered comprehensive health assessments and lifetime medical services. Tuskegee Health Benefit Program congressionally established and administered by CDC. Class action lawsuit filed by Mr. Fred Gray on behalf of the living Study participants and heirs of deceased participants.

1974 – National Research Act signed into law, creating the National Commission for the Protection of Human Subjects of Biomedical and Behavioral Research.

1974 – Federal regulations developed to review and approve research involving human subjects.

1975 – Class action suit settled. Cash payment of $37,500 to every living man with syphilis who was alive on July 23, 1973; $15,000 to the heirs of each of the deceased men with syphilis; $16,000 to every member of the class of living controls who was alive on July 23, 1973; and $5,000 to the heirs of each of the deceased controls.

1979 – The Belmont Report summarizing the basic ethical principles governing research involving humans is released by the National Commission for the Protection of Human Subjects of Biomedical and Behavioral Research.

1996 – Tuskegee Syphilis Study Legacy Committee established and report issued with their recommendations that "President Clinton publicly apologize for past government wrongdoing to the Study's living survivors, their families, and to the Tuskegee community," and that a strategy be developed "to redress the damages caused by the Study to transform its damaging legacy."

1997 – President Clinton delivers formal apology to Tuskegee Study Survivors and families. (Editor's note.)

READING

6

TWENTY YEARS OF TUSKEGEE

Eunice Rivers, Stanley H. Schuman,
Lloyd Simpson and Sidney Olansky

Eunice Rivers, R.N., was the public health nurse in Macon County, Alabama, who facilitated the Tuskegee Study. Lloyd Simpson was venereal disease field investigator for the Public Health Service. Stanley Schuman, M.D., was affiliated with the clinical investigations section of the Venereal Disease Research Laboratory in the Communicable Disease Center, Chamblee, Georgia. Sidney Olansky, M.D., was director of the laboratory. The four published the article in the U.S. Public Health Reports in 1953, more than 20 years after the Tuskegee Study began and just as penicillin was recognized as a safe and effective treatment for illness, including syphilis. The Tuskegee Study continued for nearly two more decades after this report, without employing penicillin treatment.

■ POINTS TO CONSIDER

1. Discuss the portrayal of the men who participated in the study. Do you believe their recruitment and participation throughout the study was rooted in the principle of informed consent?

2. Define the role of Eunice Rivers.

3. What elements are most important to the researchers in the study?

4. Describe ways the researchers attracted and maintained participants in the study.

5. What was the nature of the relationship between doctor and participant?

Excerpted from Eunice Rivers, Stanley H. Schuman, Lloyd Simpson and Sidney Olansky, "Twenty Years of Followup Experience in a Long-Range Medical Study," **Public Health Reports,** vol. 68, no. 4, April 1953: 391-5.

One cannot work with a group of people over a long period of time without becoming attached to them. This has been the experience of the nurse. Realizing that they do depend upon her and give her their trust, she has to help in the most ethical way to see that they get the best care.

One of the longest continued medical surveys ever conducted is the study of untreated syphilis in the male Negro. This study was begun by the Public Health Service in the fall of 1932 in Macon County, Ala., a rural area in the eastern part of the state, and is now entering its twenty-second year. This paper is the first report dealing with the nonmedical aspects of the study. The experiences recounted may be of value to those who are planning continuing studies in other fields.

ORGANIZING THE STUDY

In beginning the study, schedules of the blood-drawing clinics throughout the county were announced through every available source, including churches, schools, and community stores. The people responded willingly, and 600 patients were selected for the study – 400 who had syphilis and, for controls, 200 who did not. The patients who had syphilis were all in the latent stage; any acute cases requiring treatment were carefully screened out for standard therapy.

At Tuskegee, each of the 600 patients initially was given a complete physical examination, including chest X-ray and electro-cardiogram. Careful histories were taken and blood tests were repeated. Thereafter, each of the patients was followed up with an annual blood test and, whenever the Public Health Service physicians came to Tuskegee, physical examinations were repeated.

There have been four surveys: in 1932, 1938, 1948, and 1952. Between surveys contact with the patients was maintained through the local county health department and an especially assigned public health nurse, whose chief duties were those of followup worker on this project. The nurse also participated in a generalized public health nursing program, which gave her broad contact with the families of the patients and demonstrated that she was interested in other aspects of their welfare as well as in the project. The nurse was a native of the county, who had lived near her patients all her life, and was thoroughly familiar with their local ideas and customs.

MAINTAINING SUBJECTS

A most important phase of the study was to follow as many patients as possible to postmortem examination, in order to determine the prevalence and severity of the syphilitic disease process. Cooperation of patients with this plan was sought by offering burial assistance (through a private philanthropy, the Milbank Memorial Fund) on condition that permission be granted for autopsy. For the majority of these poor farmers such financial aid was a real boon, and often it was the only "insurance" they could hope for. The Federal Government offered physical examinations and incidental medication, such as tonics and analgesics, but was unable to provide financial assistance on a continuing basis. The Milbank Memorial Fund burial assistance made it possible to obtain a higher percentage of permissions for postmortem examinations than otherwise would have been granted.

TRANSPORTATION

Transportation to the hospital for X-rays and physical examination was furnished by the nurse. Her car was too small to bring in more than two patients at one trip; therefore, two men were scheduled for examination in the morning and two for the afternoon. During the early years of the study, when the county was strictly a rural one, the roads were very poor, some being impassable during the rainy season. Very often, the patients spent hours helping to get the car out of a mudhole. Now, with modern conveniences (telephones, electricity, cars, and good roads) the nurse's problems are fewer than in the early days.

Having a complete physical examination by a doctor in a hospital was a new experience for most of the men. Some were skeptical; others were frightened and left without an examination. Those who were brave enough to remain were very pleased. Only one objection occurred frequently: the "back shot," never again! There are those who, today, unjustifiably attribute current complaints (backaches, headaches, nervousness) to those spinal punctures.

FOLLOWUP

The patients have been followed through the years by the same nurse but by different doctors. Some doctors were liked by all the patients; others were liked by only a few. The chief factor in this was the length of time doctor and patients had to get to know each other. If the doctor's visit to the area was brief, he might not have time to learn and to understand the habits of the patients. Likewise, the patients did not have an opportunity to understand the doctor. Because of their confidence in the nurse, the patients often expressed their opinion about the doctor privately to her. She tried always to assure them that the doctor was a busy person interested in many things, but that they really were first on his program.

CULTURAL GAP

It is very important for the followup worker to understand both patient and doctor, because she must bridge the gap between the two. The doctors were concerned primarily with obtaining the most efficient and thorough medical examination possible for the group of 600 men. While they tried to give each patient the personal interest he desired, this was not always possible due to the pressure of time. Occasionally, the patient was annoyed because the doctor did not pay attention to his particular complaint. He may have believed that his favorite home remedy was more potent than the doctor's prescription. It then became the task of the nurse to convince him that the examinations were beneficial. If she failed, she might find that in the future he not only neglected to answer her letters but managed to be away from home whenever she called. Sometimes the doctor grumbled because of the seemingly poor cooperation and slowness of some of the patients; often the nurse helped in these situations simply by bridging the language barrier and by explaining to the men what the doctor wanted.

Sometimes the nurse assisted the physician by warning him beforehand about the eccentricities of the patients he was scheduled to see during the day. For example, there was the lethargic patient with early cancer of the lip who needed strong language and grim predictions to persuade him to seek medical attention. On the other hand, there was the hypochondriac who overheard the doctor mention the 45° angle of rotation of his body during the X-ray examination; the next day, the entire county was buzzing with gossip about their remarkable friend who was "still alive, walking around with his heart tilted at a 45° angle."

51

OVERCOMING FEARS

As the newness of the project wore off and fears of being hurt were relieved, the gatherings became more social. The examination became an opportunity for men from different and often isolated parts of the county to meet and exchange news. Later, the nurse's small car was replaced with a large, new, Government station wagon. The ride to and from the hospital in this vehicle with the Government emblem on the front door, chauffeured by the nurse, was a mark of distinction for many of the men who enjoyed waving to their neighbors as they drove by. They knew that they could get their pills and "spring tonic" from the nurse whenever they needed them between surveys, but they looked forward happily to having the Government doctor take their blood pressure and listen to their hearts. Those men who were advised about their diets were especially delighted, even though they would not adhere to the restrictions.

Because of the low educational status of the majority of the patients, it was impossible to appeal to them from a purely scientific approach. Therefore, various methods were used to maintain and stimulate their interest. Free medicines, burial assistance or insurance (the project being referred to as "Miss Rivers' Lodge"), free hot meals on the days of examination, transportation to and from the hospital, and an opportunity to stop in town on the return trip to shop or visit with their friends on the streets all helped.

OCCUPATIONAL STATUS

The study group was composed of farmers who owned their homes, renters who were considered permanent residents, and day laborers on farms and in sawmills. The laborers were the hardest to follow. Some of the resident farmers traveled to other sections seeking work after their own crops had been harvested, but they came back when it was time to start planting. An effort was made continually through relatives to keep informed of the patients' most recent addresses, and this information regularly has been placed in their records. During the 20 years of the study, 520 of the original 600 men have been followed consistently if living, or to autopsy. It is possible that some of the 80 now considered lost will at some time return to the county or write the nurse from distant places for medical advice.

AUTOPSIES

The excellent care given these patients was important in creating in the family a favorable attitude which eventually would lead to permission to perform an autopsy. Even in a friendly atmosphere, however, it was difficult for the nurse to approach the family, especially in the early years of the project, because she herself was uneasy about autopsies. She was pleasantly surprised to receive fine response from the families of the patients – only one refusal in 20 years and 145 autopsies obtained. Finally, the nurse realized that she and not the relatives had been hesitant and squeamish.

Sometimes the family asked questions concerning the autopsy, but offered no objections when they were assured that the body would not be harmed. If the patient had been ill for a long time and had not been able to secure any relief from his symptoms, they were anxious to know the reason. If he had died suddenly, they were anxious for some explanation.

One cannot work with a group of people over a long period of time without becoming attached to them. This has been the experience of the nurse. She has had an opportunity to know them personally. She has come to understand some of their problems and how these account for some of their peculiar reactions. The ties are stronger than simply those of patient and nurse. There is a feeling of complete confidence in what the nurse advises. Some of them bring problems beyond her province, concerning building, insurance, and other things about which she can give no specific advice. She directs them always to the best available sources of guidance. Realizing that they do depend upon her and give her their trust, she has to keep an open mind and must be careful always not to criticize, but to help in the most ethical way to see that they get the best care.

THE ETHICS OF TUSKEGEE

Tuskegee Syphilis Study Ad Hoc Advisory Panel
and Jay Katz

Ronald H. Brown, Dr. Vernal Cave, Barney H. Weeks, Dr. Jean L.Harris, Dr. Jeanne C. Sinkford and Fred Speaker served on the Subcommittee on Charge One of the Ad Hoc Advisory Panel designed to examine the ethical and scientific issues involved in the Tuskegee Syphilis Study. Their report, released April 24, 1973, delineates the subcommittee conclusions of the questions asked under Charge One: (1-A) determining whether the Tuskegee Study was justified in 1932 and (1-B) determining whether the study should have been continued when penicillin became generally available. Jay Katz, M.D., submitted reservations to the assistant secretary for health and scientific affairs concerning the panel report on Charge One.

■ **POINTS TO CONSIDER**

1. According to the Subcommittee, why was the Tuskegee Study not justified?

2. Summarize Dr. Katz' reservations about the official report.

3. How do his conclusions differ from the Subcommittee's?

4. Why does Dr. Katz criticize the medical profession?

Excerpted from the **Final Report of the Tuskegee Syphilis Study Ad Hoc Advisory Panel**, U.S. Department of Health, Education and Welfare, Public Health Service, April 24, 1973: 5-15.

The Public Health Service Study of Untreated Syphilis in the Male Negro in Macon County, Alabama, was ethically unjustified in 1932. The real issue is that the participants in this study were never informed of the availability of treatment because the investigators were never in favor of such treatment.

The Tuskegee Study was one of several investigations that were taking place in the 1930s with the ultimate objective of venereal disease control in the United States. In retrospect, the Public Health Service Study of Untreated Syphilis in the Male Negro in Macon County, Alabama, was ethically unjustified in 1932. This judgment made in 1973 about the conduct of the study in 1932 is made with the advantage of hindsight acutely sharpened over some forty years, concerning an activity in a different age with different social standards. Nevertheless, one fundamental ethical rule is that a person should not be subjected to avoidable risk of death or physical harm unless he freely and intelligently consents. There is no evidence that such consent was obtained from the participants in this study.

Because of the paucity of information available today on the manner in which the study was conceived, designed and sustained, a scientific justification for a short term demonstration study cannot be ruled out. However, the conduct of the longitudinal study as initially reported in 1936 and through the years is judged to be scientifically unsound, and its results are disproportionately meager compared with known risks to human subjects involved.

The position of the Panel must not be construed to be a general repudiation of scientific research with human subjects. It is possible that a scientific study in 1932 of untreated syphilis, properly conceived with a clear protocol and conducted with suitable subjects who fully understood the implications of their involvement, might have been justified in the pre-penicillin era. This is especially true when one considers the uncertain nature of the results of treatment of latent syphilis and the highly toxic nature of therapeutic agents then available.

TREATMENT OPTIONS BEFORE 1932

In 1932, treatment of syphilis in all stages was being provided through the use of a variety of chemotherapeutic agents including mercury, bismuth, arsphenamine, neoarsphenamine, iodides and various combinations thereof. Treatment procedures being used in the early 1930s extended over long periods of time (up to two years) and were not without hazard to the patient. As of 1932, also, treatment was widely recommended and treatment schedules specifically for late latent syphilis were published and in use. The rationale for treatment at that time was based on the clinical judgment "that the latent syphilitic patient must be regarded as a potential carrier of the disease and should be treated for the sake of the Community's health." The aims of treatment in the treatment of latent syphilis were stated to be: 1) to increase the probability of "cure" or arrest, 2) to decrease the probability of progression or relapse, 3) to control potential infectiousness from contact of the patient with adults of either sex, or in the case of women with latent syphilis, with unborn children.

ETHICS OF CONTINUATION

There is a crucial absence of evidence that patients were given a "choice" of continuing in the study once penicillin became readily available. This fact serves to amplify the magnitude of encroachment on the human lives and well-being of the participants in this study. This is especially significant when there is uncertainty as to the whole issue of "consent" of the participants.

The ethical, legal and scientific implications which are evoked from the facts presented in the previous section led the Panel to the following judgment: penicillin therapy should have been made available to the participants in this study especially as of 1953 when penicillin became generally available.

Withholding of penicillin, after it became generally available, amplified the injustice to which this group of human beings had already been subjected. The scientific merits of the Tuskegee Study are vastly overshadowed by the violation of basic ethical principles pertaining to human dignity and human life imposed on the experimental subjects.

RESERVATIONS ABOUT THE PANEL REPORT ON CHARGE I by Jay Katz

I should like to add the following findings and observations to the majority opinion:

There is ample evidence in the records available to us that the consent to participation was not obtained from the Tuskegee Syphilis Study subjects, but that instead they were exploited, manipulated and deceived. They were treated not as human subjects but as objects of research. The most fundamental reason for condemning the Tuskegee Study at its inception and throughout its continuation is not that all the subjects should have been treated, for some might not have wished to be treated, but rather that they were never fairly consulted about the research project, its consequences for them, and the alternatives available to them. Those who for reasons of intellectual incapacity could not have been so consulted should not have been invited to participate in the study in the first place.

KNOWN OUTCOMES

It was already known before the Tuskegee Syphilis Study was begun, and reconfirmed by the study itself, that persons with untreated syphilis have a higher death rate than those who have been treated. The life expectancy of at least forty subjects in the study was markedly decreased for lack of treatment.

In addition, the untreated and the "inadvertently" (using the word

57

frequently employed by the investigators) but inadequately treated subjects suffered many complications which could have been ameliorated with treatment. This fact was noted on occasion in the published reports of the Tuskegee Syphilis Study and as late as 1971. However the subjects were not apprised of this possibility.

One of the senior investigators wrote in 1936 that since "a considerable portion of the infected Negro population remained untreated during the entire course of syphilis, an unusual opportunity arose to study the untreated syphilitic patient from the beginning of the disease to the death of the infected person." Throughout, the investigators seem to have confused the study with an "experiment in nature." But syphilis was not a condition for which no beneficial treatment was available, calling for experimentation to learn more about the condition in the hope of finding a remedy. The persistence of the syphilitic disease from which the victims of the Tuskegee Study suffered resulted from the unwillingness or incapacity of society to mobilize the necessary resources for treatment. The investigators, the U.S. Public Health Service (USPHS), and the private foundations who gave support to this study should not have exploited this situation in the fashion they did. Unless they could have guaranteed knowledgeable participation by the subjects, they all should have disappeared from the research scene or else utilized their limited research resources for therapeutic ends. Instead, the investigators believed that the persons involved in the Tuskegee Study would never seek out treatment; a completely unwarranted assumption which ultimately led the investigators deliberately to obstruct the opportunity for treatment from a number of the participants.

PRINCIPLE OF MORALITY

In theory if not in practice, it has long been "a principle of medical and surgical morality never to perform on man an experiment which might be harmful to any extent, even though the result might be highly advantageous to science" (Claude Bernard 1865), at least without the knowledgeable consent of the subject. This was one basis on which the German physicians who had conducted medical experiments in concentration camps were tried by the Nuremberg Military Tribunal for crimes against humanity. Testimony at their trial by official representatives of the American Medical Association clearly suggested that research like the Tuskegee Syphilis Study would have been intolerable in this country or anywhere in the civilized world. Yet the Tuskegee Syphilis

> ## THEY WERE BETRAYED
>
> So today America does remember the hundreds of men used in research without their knowledge and consent. We remember them and their family members. Men who were poor and African American, without resources and with few alternatives, they believed they had found hope when they were offered free medical care by the United States Public Health Service. They were betrayed.
>
> Excerpted from the remarks of Bill Clinton from the White House, May 16, 1997.

Study was continued after the Nuremberg findings and the Nuremberg Code had been widely disseminated to the medical community. Moreover, the study was not reviewed in 1966 after the Surgeon General of the U.S. Public Health Service (USPHS) promulgated his guidelines for the ethical conduct of research, even though this study was carried on within the purview of his department.

UNHEEDED WARNING

The Tuskegee Syphilis Study finally was reviewed in 1969. A lengthier transcript of the proceedings, not quoted by the majority, reveals that one of the five members of the reviewing committee repeatedly emphasized that a moral obligation existed to provide treatment for the "patients." His plea remained unheeded. Instead the Committee, which was in part concerned with the possibility of adverse criticism, seemed to be reassured by the observation that "if we established good liaison with the local medical society, there would be no need to answer criticism."

The controversy over the effectiveness and the dangers of arsenic and heavy metal treatment in 1932 and of penicillin treatment when it was introduced as a method of therapy is beside the point. For the real issue is that the participants in this study were never informed of the availability of treatment, because the investigators were never in favor of such treatment. Throughout the study, the responsibility rested heavily on the shoulders of the investigators to make every effort to apprise the subjects of what could be done for them if they so wished. In 1937 the then

Surgeon General of the USPHS wrote: "for late syphilis no blanket prescription can be written. Each patient is a law unto himself. For every syphilis patient, late and early, a careful physical examination is necessary before starting treatment and examinations should be repeated frequently during its course." Even prior to that, in 1932, ranking USPHS physicians stated in a series of articles that adequate treatment "will afford a practical, if not complete guarantee of freedom from the development of any late lesions."

IGNORING THE ISSUE

In conclusion, I note sadly that the medical profession, through its national association, its many individual societies, and its journals, has on the whole not reacted to this study except by ignoring it. One lengthy editorial appeared in the October 1972 issue of the *Southern Medical Journal* which exonerated the study and chastised the "irresponsible press" for bringing it to public attention. When will we take seriously our responsibilities, particularly to the disadvantaged in our midst who so consistently throughout history have been the first to be selected for human research?

READING

8

TUSKEGEE AGAIN: DENYING POOR WOMEN AND INFANTS LIFE-SAVING TREATMENTS

Public Citizen

In a letter to Secretary of Health and Human Services Donna Shalala, signed by Peter Lurie, M.D., Sidney M. Wolfe, M.D., of the Public Citizen's Health Research group, Wilbert Jordan, M.D., Chairman , Black Los Angeles AIDS Consortium, George J. Annas, JD, MPH, Boston University School of Public Health, Michael Grodin, M.D., Boston University School of Public Health, and George Silver, M.D., Yale University School of Medicine, Public Citizen charged that experiments conducted with women in developing countries, funded by the U.S. government, denied women and infants live-saving treatments. The studies, mostly in developing countries, attempt to discover new ways to reduce mother-to-infant transmission (MTI) of Human Immuno-Deficiency Virus (HIV). A regimen (tested in the U.S.), referred to as Protocol 076, was discovered to reduce MIT by perhaps as much as two-thirds. With this knowledge, Public Citizen contends that it is unethical to employ placebo arms in the foreign studies which deny women treatment of Protocol 076, known to reduce MTI of HIV. Public Citizen is a nonprofit organization in Washington, D.C. Founded by consumer advocate Ralph Nader in 1971, the organization seeks to promote safe and healthy work, consumer and natural environments.

■ POINTS TO CONSIDER

1. Define the original Protocol 076. Where was the study conducted? What were the impacts of the results?

2. Analyze the designs of the new experiments abroad. Can you draw parallels between the subjects and experiment in Tuskegee with those of the HIV experiments?

3. Why do the authors of the letter to Secretary Shalala contend that different standards of care exist between the industrialized world and the developing world?

4. After reading the letter, summarize your concerns about the authors' contentions and/or the study's designs.

5. Why do the authors air their concerns to the Secretary of Health and Human Services?

Excerpted from a letter by **Public Citizen** to Secretary of Health and Human Services, Donna Shalala, April 22, 1997. **Public Citizen**, 1600 20th Street, N.W., Washington, D.C. 20009, (202) 588-1000; E-mail: public_citizen@citizen.org.

It is a violation of basic research ethics to assert that the failure to prevent HIV infection is somehow justified by the potential for preventing future HIV infections.

It is projected that by the year 2000, six million pregnant women will be infected with HIV, primarily in Asia and sub-Saharan Africa. In the absence of prophylaxis, transmission from HIV-infected mother to infant occurs in between 13% and 48% of pregnancies, with rates in developing countries typically being higher than in industrialized countries. In the U.S., 933 AIDS cases involving mother-to-infant transmission were reported in 1994, and, at least in the period prior to Protocol 076, an estimated 1,000 to 2,000 HIV infections via this route were estimated to occur annually.

DECLINE IN TRANSMISSION

The single most important advance in the prevention of HIV transmission from mother to infant has been the AZT regimen demonstrated to be effective in Protocol 076. Beginning in April 1991, researchers at a large number of sites in the U.S. and France conducted a randomized, double-blind, placebo-controlled trial in which the treatment group received oral AZT beginning at 14-34 weeks of pregnancy and intravenous AZT during labor. The newborns received oral AZT beginning shortly after birth and continuing for six weeks. In order to reduce the likelihood that subjects in one of the two study arms were benefiting or being harmed compared to those in the other study arm, a Data and Safety Monitoring Board was constituted and was scheduled to review the interim results on three occasions. At the first interim analysis, in December 1993, the findings were so striking that the study was stopped and AZT prophylaxis was offered to all women and infants still in the study. Providing AZT thus became the standard of care for HIV-infected pregnant women.

In November 1996, the Protocol 076 researchers published updated data describing their findings. In the placebo group, 22.6% of the infants of the HIV-infected mothers had become infected with HIV, compared to only 7.6% of those treated with AZT, a reduction of approximately two-thirds. The provision of AZT to HIV-positive pregnant women is still the only intervention for any group at risk for HIV to be proved effective in reducing the number of new HIV infections in a randomized, controlled trial. The impact on actual clinical outcomes in the U.S. has been dramatic. Three recent reports document decreases in HIV transmission from HIV-infected mother to infant of 50% or more.

FUTURE EXPLORATION, EXPLOITATION

The studies involving AZT generally explore the optimal dose and timing of AZT administration. A total of 17 studies appear, two of which are in the U.S. The remainder are in developing countries, primarily in Africa: three studies each in Cote d'Ivoire and Uganda, two studies each in Thailand, Tanzania and South Africa, and one study each in Ethiopia, Burkina Faso, Malawi, Zimbabwe, Kenya, and the Dominican Republic. Two studies are occurring at more than one site. We are also aware of an additional study in Malawi that has been completed. This study enrolled 2,094 women in an National Institutes of Health (NIH)-funded study of vaginal washing. Of the remaining studies, two have been completed: the NIH-funded study by John Hopkins University in Malawi, the data from which are now being analyzed, and the NIH-funded Aids Clinical Test Group ACTG 185 in the U.S., which was terminated early when the transmission rate from the women, all of whom received AZT, to their infants was about 4.8%, even lower than in the treatment group in Protocol 076.

The two studies in the U.S. both provide anti-HIV drugs to all study subjects, as does one of the studies in the developing countries, that conducted by Harvard University in Thailand using NIH funds. This leaves 15 randomized, controlled trials, all in developing countries in which some or all HIV-infected pregnant women are denied effective prophylaxis. Seven of the 15 studies are funded by the NIH and two are funded by the Centers for Disease Control and Prevention (CDC). A total of 9,055 women are enrolled in the nine U.S.-funded studies, 2,903 of whom will receive placebos and 3,780 of whom will receive regimens not proved effective in randomized, controlled trials. The remaining six studies are funded by the ANRS (the French equivalent of the NIH; two studies), the United Nations AIDS program, the University of Natal and Department of Health in South Africa, and groups from Denmark and Belgium. In these six studies, in which 5,160 women are enrolled, 1,855 will receive placebos and 1,490 will receive regimens that have not been proven effective.

UNNECESSARY DEATHS

It is possible to calculate the number of infants who will unnecessarily become infected with HIV in these unethical studies, assuming that the regimens not yet proved effective are indeed not effective. In the 15 studies, a total of 10,028 women will not receive effective prophylaxis such as AZT. Fifteen percent of them (22.6% - 7.6%) will give birth to infants with HIV infection that could have been prevented by AZT or a similarly effective regimen – a total of 1,504 preventable deaths. Of these, 1,002 will occur in U.S.-funded studies and 502 will occur in those funded by foreign governments or the United Nations AIDS program. Even if only the placebo arms of the studies are considered, a total of 714 preventable HIV infections, 435 of them in U.S.-funded studies, will occur.

It is a violation of basic research ethics to assert that the failure to prevent HIV infection in these studies is somehow justified by the potential for preventing future HIV infections based on data that may be generated in this research. As the World Medical Association has declared: "Concern for the interests of the subject must always prevail over the interests of science and society." In part, this ethical principle was enunciated to prevent the more powerful from using theoretical future gains to place the less powerful at risk in the present. Indeed, the very fact that the subjects of these studies are persons of color from impoverished, mostly post-colonial societies underscores the dangers of such rationalizations.

GAINS ON THE BACKS OF THE POOR

Clearly, any simpler or less expensive prophylactic regimen that was as effective and safe as that used in Protocol 076 would be rapidly adopted in the industrialized world, and while it is true that many of the strategies being tested in these studies are less expensive than that used in Protocol 076, they may still be unaffordable in developing countries. There is, therefore, no guarantee that women and infants in developing countries will even benefit from any knowledge gained from this research. As a recent editorial entitled "Scientific Imperialism" in the *British Medical Journal* proclaimed: "If they won't benefit from the findings, poor people in the developing world shouldn't be used in research."

Defenders of these studies will no doubt argue that the subjects are being provided the "standard of care" practiced in these developing countries, which is to say regimens that have not been proven effective or no treatment at all. (Of course, this coerces potential subjects to enroll, as outside of the study they stand essentially no chance of obtaining proven effective prophylaxis.) Yet the standard of care in the U.S. – Protocol 076 – can be delivered in the research setting in developing countries and is essentially being provided as one of the arms of the only developing country study here that is ethical: Harvard University's NIH-funded study of various regimens of AZT prophylaxis in Thailand. As NIH Director Harold Varmus stated at a recent meeting regarding the Alaska needle exchange study, clinical trials funded by the NIH should comply with a higher ethical standard. Instead, many of these studies subscribe to a kind of lowest common denominator ethics in which the abominable state of health care in developing countries is used to justify withholding life-saving interventions.

FAULTY ETHICAL REVIEW

Incredibly, most of these studies have, to the best of our knowledge, passed ethical review by committees both in the developing country and in the West, providing further proof of the inadequacy of the current review system. We believe that the CDC-funded studies have passed review at the CDC itself, but do not know whether NIH's Office for Protection from Research Risks reviewed the NIH-funded studies. (The University researchers would also have been required to seek the formal approval of the Institutional Review Boards at their own institutions.) These events also demonstrate that the approval by a developing country ethics committee, while essential, is not sufficient to guarantee an ethical study. Developing country committee members, most of whom are likely to be researchers, are usually from social classes higher than the study subjects and may not be able to adequately reflect the subjects' interests. For developing country researchers, involvement in international studies offers obvious benefits in prestige and, perhaps, in salary.

It is true that providing AZT according to Protocol 076 or other similar regimens to all subjects could lower the number of new HIV infections to the point that it may be more difficult to statistically demonstrate differences between the study groups. Indeed, this is the crux of the researchers' conflict of interest: it is the potential for large numbers of infections among women denied AZT that makes the developing countries "preferable" as study sites to industrialized countries where AZT would have to be provided to all HIV-positive pregnant women. The solution to this conflict of interest is not to create a research double-standard; it is to spend the money for larger studies, perhaps at multiple sites in the industrialized or developing worlds, with appropriate informed consent. For example, one study arm could receive AZT and the other AZT and the experimental prophylactic regimen. With the public scrutiny that will accompany these studies, as well as the HIV vaccine studies that may follow, researchers cannot afford to be unethical.

OBSERVING THE NUREMBERG CODE

The failure to provide effective prophylaxis to all women in these research studies can also not be explained by the cost of providing AZT in the research setting; after all, both the U.S. studies offer anti-HIV drugs to all subjects and seven of the studies outside the U.S. provide some form of AZT prophylaxis in some study treatment arms. The wholesale cost of the Protocol 076 regimen has been estimated at $614 and $895 per person. In the context of the hundreds of thousands, if not millions, of dollars being spent on these studies, this is a modest amount of money. In any event, the manufacturer of AZT has in the past customarily provided the medication for these trials free of charge.

Following World War II, the Nuremberg Code of research conduct was adopted. In this 50th year since the commencement of the Nuremberg doctor trials, it is disheartening in the extreme that, at a minimum, four of the ten principles of the Code have been abrogated in this research.

Principle Two: "The experiment should be such as to yield fruitful results for the good of society, unprocurable by other methods or means of study, and not random and unnecessary in nature."

Principle Four: "The experiment should be so conducted as to avoid all unnecessary physical and mental suffering and injury."

Principle Five: "No experiment should be conducted where there is an a priori reason to believe that death or disabling injury will occur except, perhaps, in those experiments where the experimental physicians also serve as subjects."

Principle Seven: "Proper preparations should be made and adequate facilities provided to protect the experimental subject against even remote possibilities of injury, disability, or death."

We request that you immediately order the researchers in these studies to provide effective prophylaxis to all subjects in these studies and that you pressure the foreign governments who are also funding these studies to do likewise. We also request that you immediately ask the Health and Human Services Office of the Inspector General to launch an investigation into how these U.S.-funded studies received ethical approval, and into possible violations of federal law. We are confident that you would not wish the reputation of your department to be stained with the blood of foreign infants.

READING

9

VALUED RESEARCH CONTINUES:
DEVELOPING LIFE-SAVING TREATMENTS FOR MOTHERS AND INFANTS

Department of Health and Human Services

In a letter responding to the concerns of Public Citizen, *Secretary of Health and Human Services Donna Shalala defends studies in foreign countries on maternal-infant transmission of HIV. The following is a supplement to Shalala's response letter, signed by Harold Varmus, director of the National Institutes of Health and David Satcher, director of the Centers for Disease Control and Prevention. The summary examines their view of needs for developing countries in discovering ways to reduce maternal-infant HIV transmission, and the ways in which the studies funded by their organizations accommodate these needs.*

■ **POINTS TO CONSIDER**

1. Summarize the reasons why AZT (ZDV) treatment regimens in the U.S. to prevent mother-to-infant transmission are not feasible in the developing world.

2. Define the purpose of maternal-infant transmission studies in the developing world. Why do researchers insist upon placebo arms in these studies?

3. Describe the differences between the CDC and NIH Studies in Thailand and the significance of these differences.

4. Evaluate the contention that it is unethical to employ a treatment regimen from the industrialized world for studies in poor countries.

Excerpted from the enclosure from a letter from Secretary of Health and Human Services Donna Shalala to **Public Citizen**, July 15, 1997. Harold Varmus and David Satcher, "The Conduct of Clinical Trials of Maternal-Infant Transmissions of HIV," Supported by the United States Department of Health and Human Services in Developing Countries, July 1997.

The studies have the potential to be of enormous value to the developing countries and are scientifically well-founded and ethically acceptable. To evaluate interventions that they could not implement realistically would be exploitive of those in the participant country.

For the past three years the United States Department of Health and Human Services (HHS), through its National Institutes of Health (NIH) and Centers for Disease Control and Prevention (CDC), has been engaged in the development and conduct of clinical trials designed to identify feasible interventions for preventing maternal-infant transmission of HIV in developing countries. The Director of NIH, the Director of CDC, and other senior scientists and administrators within the NIH and CDC, at the request of the Secretary of HHS, conducted a thorough assessment of the previous reviews of the needs, resources, and health care capacities of these developing countries and the process of scientific development and ethical evaluation leading up to and guiding the current conduct of these clinical trials. As an added measure, comments of a number of experts in biomedical ethics and the biosciences outside of NIH and CDC were also sought and considered. Based on this assessment, NIH and CDC have determined that, although these are complex matters, the studies have the potential to be of enormous value to the developing countries and are scientifically well-founded and ethically acceptable.

THE NEED

One regimen of anti-retroviral therapy has been shown to reduce substantially the likelihood of maternal-infant transmission of HIV. The identification of this successful regimen was the result of the National Institutes of Health's AIDS Clinical Trials Group Protocol 076 (ACTG 076 or 076) in 1994. In spite of this knowledge, approximately 1,000 HIV-infected infants are born each day, the vast majority of them in developing countries. This occurs, in part, because the regimen proven to be effective is simply not feasible as a standard of prevention in much of the developing world.

There are two reasons for this lack of feasibility. First, to follow the regimen that has proven efficacy requires that the women be reached early in prenatal care; be tested for and counseled concerning their HIV status; comply with a lengthy oral treatment regimen; receive intravenous administration of the anti-retroviral zidovudine (ZDV or AZT) during labor and delivery; and refrain from breast-feeding. Additionally, the newborns must receive six weeks of oral AZT therapy. During and after the time the mother and infant are treated with AZT, both must be carefully monitored for adverse effects of exposure to this drug. In the poor countries that are the sites of these studies, these requirements could seldom be achieved, even under the infrequent circumstance when women present early enough for the screening and care requirements of the 076 therapeutic regimen to be implemented. Second, the wholesale drug costs for the AZT in the 076 regimen are estimated to be in excess of $800, an amount far greater than these developing countries could afford as standard care.

In June 1994, after the results of ACTG 076 were released, the World Health Organization (WHO) convened a group of researchers and public health practitioners from around the world in Geneva. This international panel called for the use of the 076 regimen in the industrialized world, where it is feasible, but immediately called for the exploration of alternative regimens that could be used in the developing world, stating that logistical issues and cost would preclude the widespread application of the 076 regimen.

THE STUDY DESIGNS

The NIH- and CDC-supported studies of maternal-infant transmission of HIV in developing countries are designed to meet the critical need just described. The panel convened by WHO in Geneva stated:

Most of the maternal-infant transmission (MTI) transmission of HIV occurs in the developing world, where the ZDV regimen used in ACTG 076 is not applicable because of its cost and operational requirements. In those parts of the world, the choice of a placebo for the control group of a randomized trial would be appropriate as there is currently no effective alternative for HIV-infected pregnant women.

For each individual study there has been careful consideration of the specific needs of and treatment feasibility within the country in which it would be implemented. NIH, CDC, collaborating U.S. institutions, and the host countries will continue to monitor each study and any changes in the countries that may have an impact on study design. It is an unfortunate fact that the current standard of perinatal care for the HIV-infected pregnant women in the sites of the studies does not include any HIV prophylactic intervention at all. Nor does the standard of care for these HIV-infected women include the combination therapies recommended and used for some HIV-infected women in the U.S. However, the inclusion of this regrettable, but real, performance-site standard in the form of placebo controls provides the direct comparison of standard and new intervention that is needed to form the basis for rational policy decisions and will result in the most rapid, accurate, and reliable answer to the question of the value of the intervention being studied compared to the local standard of care.

RESEARCH PROTECTIONS

Arguments against the NIH- and CDC-supported studies appear to rest on the proposition that it is unethical to conduct a clinical trial unless it offers all participants a chance to receive an effective intervention if such is available anywhere in the world, even if it is not available at the site of the clinical trial. Ideally, this would be so for all clinical trials for all therapies. But the reality is that often it is not possible. The very purpose of the NIH- and CDC-supported studies of maternal-infant transmission of HIV in developing countries is to identify interventions other than those of 076 and we agree with the WHO Geneva panel's recommendation that:

It should be emphasized that the results of ACTG 076 are only directly applicable to a specific population. Moreover, the ZDV regimen employed in the ACTG 076 study has a number of features (cost, logistical issues, among others) which limit its general applicability. Therefore, no global recommendations regarding use of ZDV to prevent MTI transmission of HIV can be made.

The WHO guidelines clearly indicate that the in-country health care capabilities of each country in which maternal-infant HIV transmission research is to be conducted must be used to define the type of research which is ethical and therefore permissible in that country. If a country will be able to afford only very minimal increments in the resources directed toward improved perinatal care for HIV-infected pregnant women and their children, then trials like those focused on vitamin A and other micronutrients are ethical, permissible, and desirable.

STUDIES IN THAILAND

The CDC-Thai study will determine how well tolerated and how effective a very simple AZT regimen is in a population of women who are infected with a subtype of HIV predominantly different from that observed in the U.S. and who also have co-factors for transmission that may differ from those seen in American populations. Because it is a two-arm, placebo-controlled clinical trial, the CDC-Thai study will provide rapid answers to many of the important questions. It will also enable the Ministry of Health and physicians in Thailand to make better-informed decisions about the use of a much-simplified AZT regimen for general use in HIV-infected pregnant women.

Complementing the CDC-Thai study is an NIH-Thai study to determine how much additional benefit, as compared to how much additional cost and adverse effect, is occasioned by small increments in treatment complexity. The NIH-Thai study has four arms, each a modest increment over the treatment arm in the CDC-Thai study. However, even the most complex arm of the NIH-Thai study is not identical to the treatment arm of 076. The NIH-Thai study will benefit from the baseline that is established by the CDC-Thai study.

Since the NIH-Thai study provides some level of AZT to all participants, the data from the CDC-Thai study would be particularly important for interpretation of results if the outcomes were the same for each of the four arms. Taken together, these two studies will provide a broad range of information about the likely value of AZT as a strategy to interrupt maternal-infant transmission of HIV.

ETHICS AND EXPLOITATION

To evaluate interventions that they could not implement realistically would be exploitive of those in the participant country since there would be no likelihood of meeting requirement 15 of the Guidelines that obliges:

...any product developed through such research will be made reasonably available to the inhabitants of the host community or country at the completion of successful testing...

Therefore, we have determined that the more compelling ethical argument is against using a regimen that if found to be superior in the study could not possibly be used in the prevention of maternal-infant transmission of HIV in the host country. Turning once again to Malawi for example, health officials there refused to permit the conduct of a study involving a full course regimen of AZT (such as that used in ACTG 076) because they believed it would be unethical to undertake such a study in Malawi given that its very limited resources and poor health infrastructure make the introduction of AZT as standard treatment for HIV-infected pregnant women unfeasible. Instead, the health officials wanted research on alternative treatment approaches that might reduce maternal-infant transmission of HIV.

The justification and ethical foundation for the NIH- and CDC-supported studies incorporate the reality that the clinical trials are examining other alternatives that could actually be used for the majority of HIV-infected pregnant women and mothers in the countries in which the clinical trials are being carried out. The process of ethical review of these trials has been rigorous. It has included community and scientific participation and the application of the U.S. rules for the protection of human research subjects in reviews by the relevant institutional review boards in the U.S. and in the countries where the clinical trials are carried out. Support from local governments has been obtained, and each active study has been and will continue to be reviewed by an independent Data and Safety Monitoring Board. These studies are in compliance with broadly accepted principles of ethics of international research, in which the need to take into account the reality of available and feasible health care is a consideration of substantial importance.

NEEDS AND BENEFITS

In summary, these studies all address an urgent need in the countries in which they are being conducted. They have been developed with extensive in-country input and participation, and they are consistent with widely accepted principles and guidelines of bioethics. Our perspective and our decision to support these trials rest heavily on local support and approval. In this regard, we point to the words of Edward K. Mbidde, Chair, AIDS Research Committee, Uganda Cancer Institute, in a letter, dated May 8, 1997, to the Director of NIH:

These are Ugandan studies conducted by Ugandan investigators

73

on Ugandans. [Elsewhere in the letter he discusses Ugandan ethical review.] Due to lack of resources we have been sponsored by organizations like yours [NIH]. We are grateful that you have been able to do so. There is a mix up of issues here which needs to be clarified. It is not the NIH conducting studies in Uganda but Ugandans conducting their study on their people for the good of their people.

The issues surrounding these studies are, indeed, complex and subject to some disagreement. However, final judgments about their appropriateness must be heavily weighted in favor of decisions made at the local level, as long as those decisions are consistent with international standards and those of the U.S. We know of no other way to realistically and rapidly address the gravity of mother-to-infant transmission of HIV in the developing world and the current lack of a proven, feasible intervention against it, than to continue the studies on which our two agencies have embarked.

WHAT IS
ETHNOCENTRIC BIAS?

This activity may be used as an individualized study guide for students in libraries and resource centers or as a discussion catalyst in small group and classroom discussions.

Many readers are unaware that written material usually expresses an opinion or bias. The skill to read with insight and understanding requires the ability to detect different kinds of bias. *Political bias, race bias, sex bias, ethnocentric bias* and *religious bias* are five basic kinds of opinions expressed in editorials and literature that attempt to persuade. This activity will focus on ethnocentric bias defined in the glossary below.

Five Kinds of Editorial Opinion or Bias

Sex Bias — The expression of dislike for and/or feeling of superiority over a person because of gender or sexual preference.

Race Bias — The expression of dislike for and/or feeling of superiority over a racial group.

Ethnocentric Bias — The expression of a belief that one's own group, race, religion, culture, or nation is superior. Ethnocentric persons judge others by their own standards and values.

Political Bias — The expression of political opinions and attitudes about government-related issues on the local, state, national or international level.

Religious Bias — The expression of a religious belief or attitude.

Guidelines

Read through the following statements and decide which ones represent ethnocentric bias. Evaluate each statement by using the method indicated below.

- Mark (E) for statements that reflect any ethnocentric bias.
- Mark (F) for any factual statements.
- Mark (O) for statements of opinion that reflect other kinds of opinion or bias.
- Mark (N) for any statements that you are not sure about.

_____ 1. The Public Health Service Study of Untreated Syphilis in the Male Negro in Macon County, Alabama, was ethically unjustified.

_____ 2. The real issue is that the participants in this study were never informed of the availability of treatment because the investigators were never in favor of such treatment.

_____ 3. Penicillin therapy should have been made available to the participants in this study, especially as of 1953 when penicillin became generally available.

_____ 4. Consent to participate was not obtained from the Tuskegee Syphilis Study subjects, but instead they were exploited, manipulated and deceived.

_____ 5. Christians are usually generous to other people.

_____ 6. Jews are very sympathetic to others.

_____ 7. Blacks are of equal intelligence to the average person.

_____ 8. Immigrants may sometimes prove disloyal to the government.

_____ 9. Minority groups cannot be trusted to always be self-reliant.

_____10. Poor people need to be more resourceful.

_____11. Latin people are highly emotional.

_____12. Religious people are more considerate of others.

_____13. Poor black people in inner cities lack motivation and self-reliance.

_____14. White people are usually intolerant of others.

CHAPTER 3

MILITARY RESEARCH AND HUMAN SUBJECTS

77

READING

10

QUESTIONS OF CONSENT:
50 YEARS OF MILITARY HUMAN EXPERIMENTATION

U.S. Senate Committee on Veterans' Affairs Staff

The following was prepared by the majority staff of the U.S. Senate Committee on Veterans' Affairs. The report was the result of a work of Diana Zuckerman, Ph.D., and Patricia Olson, D.V.M., Ph.D., entitled "Is Military Research Hazardous to Veterans' Health? Lessons from the Persian Gulf," May 6, 1994 and the contributions of Senate Veterans' Committee Staff after hearings on the subject of military research in 1994. The hearings were called by then chair John D. Rockefeller IV (D-W.V.) and took place on May 6,1994 and August 5, 1994.

■ **POINTS TO CONSIDER**

1. Why does the report question some military experiments with human subjects?

2. Examine the protocol that guides human experimentation for the military from a.) the military's perspective b.) Nuremberg and Helsinki guidelines.

3. Describe the types of experiments that the report calls to question.

4. Suggest why the issue of informed consent may be pertinent in light of the health issues facing Gulf War veterans in the 1990s.

Excerpted from the Senate Veterans' Committee Staff Report, **Is Military Research Hazardous to Veterans' Health? Lessons of a Half Century**, December 8, 1994.

Current law prevents the Department of Defense from using Federal funds for research involving the use of human experimental subjects, unless the subject gives informed consent in advance.

During the last 50 years, hundreds of thousands of military personnel have been involved in human experimentation and other intentional exposures conducted by the Department of Defense (DOD), often without a servicemember's knowledge or consent. In some cases, soldiers who consented to serve as human subjects found themselves participating in experiments quite different from those described at the time they volunteered. For example, thousands of World War II veterans who originally volunteered to "test summer clothing" in exchange for extra leave time, found themselves in gas chambers testing the effects of mustard gas and lewisite. Additionally, soldiers were sometimes ordered by commanding officers to "volunteer" to participate in research or face dire consequences. For example, several Persian Gulf War veterans interviewed by Committee staff reported that they were ordered to take experimental vaccines during Operation Desert Shield or face prison.

LAUDABLE GOALS, QUESTIONABLE CONDUCT

The goals of many of the military experiments and exposures were very appropriate. For example, some experiments were intended to provide important information about how to protect U.S. troops from nuclear, biological, and chemical weapons or other dangerous substances during wartime. In the Persian Gulf War, U.S. troops were intentionally exposed to an investigational vaccine that was intended to protect them against biological warfare, and they were given pyridostigmine bromide pills in an experimental protocol intended to protect them against chemical warfare.

However, some of the studies that have been conducted had more questionable motives. For example, the DOD conducted numerous "man-break" tests, exposing soldiers to chemical weapons in order to determine the exposure level that would cause a casualty, i.e., "break a man." Similarly, hundreds of soldiers were subjected to hallucinogens in experimental programs conducted by the DOD in participation with, or sponsored by, the CIA. These servicemembers often unwittingly participated as human subjects in tests for drugs intended for mind-control or behavior modification, often without their knowledge or consent. Although the ultimate goal of those experiments was to provide information that would help U.S. military and intelligence efforts, most Americans would agree that the use of soldiers as unwitting guinea pigs in experiments that were designed to harm them, at least temporarily, is not ethical.

Whether the goals of these experiments and exposures were worthy or not, these experiences put hundred of thousands of U.S. servicemembers at risk, and may have caused lasting harm to many individuals.

QUESTIONS OF INFORMED CONSENT

Every year, thousands of experiments utilizing human subjects are still being conducted by, or on behalf of, the DOD. Many of these ongoing experiments have very appropriate goals, such as obtaining information for preventing, diagnosing, and treating various diseases and disabilities acquired during military service. Although military personnel are the logical choice as human subjects for such research, it is questionable whether the military hierarchy allows for individuals in subordinate positions of power to refuse to participate in military experiments. It is also questionable whether those who participated as human subjects in military research were given adequate information to fully understand the potential benefits and risks of the experiments. Moreover, the evidence suggests that they have not been adequately monitored for adverse health effects after the experimental protocols end.

Veterans who become ill or disabled due to military service are eligible to receive priority access to medical care at VA medical facilities and to receive monthly compensation checks. In order to qualify, they must demonstrate that their illness or disability was associated with their military service. Veterans who did not know that they were exposed to dangerous substances while they were in the military, therefore, would not apply for or receive the medical care or compensation that they are entitled to. Moreover, even if they know about the exposure, it would be difficult or impossible to prove if the military has not kept adequate records. It is therefore crucial that the VA learn as much as possible about the potential exposures, and that the DOD assume responsibility for providing such information to veterans and to the VA.

Reprinted with permission from the **Star Tribune,** Minneapolis.

NUREMBERG CODE

The Nuremberg Code is a 10-point declaration governing human experimentation, developed by the Allies after World War II in response to inhumane experiments conducted by Nazi scientists and physicians. The Code states that voluntary and informed consent is absolutely essential from all human subjects who participate in research, whether during war or peace.

There is no provision in the Nuremberg Code that allows a country to waive informed consent for military personnel or veterans who serve as human subjects in experiments during wartime or in experiments that are conducted because of threat of war. However, the DOD has recently argued that wartime experimental requirements differ from peacetime requirements for informed consent. According to the Pentagon, "In all peacetime applications, we believe strongly in informed consent and its ethical foundations...But military combat is different." The DOD argued that informed consent should be waived for investigational drugs that could possibly save a soldier's life, avoid endangerment of the other personnel in his unit, and accomplish the combat mission.

HELSINKI

More than a decade after the development of the Nuremberg Code, the World Medical Association prepared recommendations as a guide to doctors using human subjects in biomedical research. As a result, in 1964 the Eighteenth World Medical Assembly met in Helsinki, Finland, and adopted recommendations to be used as an ethical code by all medical doctors conducting biomedical research with human subjects. This code, referred to as the Declaration of Helsinki, was revised in 1975, 1983, and 1989. It differs from the Nuremberg Code in certain important respects. The Declaration of Helsinki distinguishes between clinical (therapeutic) and nonclinical (nontherapeutic) biomedical research, and addresses "proxy consent" for human subjects who are legally incompetent, such as children or adults with severe physical or mental disabilities. Proxy consent for legally competent military personnel who participate in military research is not considered appropriate under the Nuremberg Code or the Declaration of Helsinki.

Current law prevents the Department of Defense from using Federal funds for research involving the use of human experimental subjects, unless the subject gives informed consent in advance. This law applies regardless of whether the research is intended to benefit the subject.

MUSTARD GAS AND LEWISITE

According to a report published by the Institute of Medicine last year, approximately 60,000 military personnel were used as human subjects in the 1940s to test two chemical agents, mustard gas and lewisite. Most of these subjects were not informed of the nature of the experiments and never received medical followup after their participation in the research. Additionally, some of these human subjects were threatened with imprisonment at Fort Leavenworth if they discussed these experiments with anyone, including their wives, parents, and family doctors.

SEVENTH-DAY ADVENTISTS

Many experiments that tested various biological agents on human subjects, referred to as Operation Whitecoat, were carried out at Fort Detrick, MD, in the 1950s. The human subjects originally consisted of volunteer enlisted men. However, after the enlisted men staged a sitdown strike to obtain more information about the dangers of the

CLOUDS OF SECRECY

The army began a program in 1949 to assess the nation's vulnerability to attack with biological weapons. During the next 20 years, biological and chemical agents were released over hundreds of populated areas around the country. Tests were conducted in Hawaii and Alaska, San Francisco, St. Louis, Minneapolis, and many other cities. Some tests were narrowly focused, as when bacteria were released in the New York City subway system and in Washington National Airport. The purpose was to see how the bacteria spread and survived as people went about normal activities.

The Pentagon maintained that the bacteria and chemicals used in these tests were harmless. Described as simulants, they were intended to mimic more lethal bacteria and chemicals that might be used in actual warfare. Yet increases in infections among people in some of the testing areas were reported from the outset.

Excerpted from the testimony of Leonard A. Cole before the Subcommittee on Legislation and National Security of the House of Representatives Committee on Government Operations, September 28, 1994.

biological tests, Seventh-Day Adventists who were conscientious objectors were recruited for the studies. Because these individuals did not believe in engaging in actual combat, they instead volunteered to be human subjects in military research projects that tested various infectious agents. At least 2,200 military personnel who were Seventh-Day Adventists volunteered for biological testing during the 1950s through the 1970s.

Unlike most of the studies discussed in this report, Operation Whitecoat was truly voluntary. Leaders of the Seventh-Day Adventist Church described these human subjects as "conscientious participants," rather than "conscientious objectors," because they were willing to risk their lives by participating in research rather than by fighting a war.

DUGWAY PROVING GROUND

Dugway Proving Ground is a military testing facility located approximately 80 miles from Salt Lake City. For several decades,

Dugway has been the site of testing for various chemical and biological agents. From 1951 through 1969, hundreds, perhaps thousands of open-air tests using bacteria and viruses that cause disease in humans, animals, and plants were conducted at Dugway. In 1968, approximately 6,400 sheep died following the intentional release of a deadly nerve gas from a plane. According to a veterinarian who evaluated the sick and dying sheep, there was little doubt that the sheep had been poisoned with nerve gas.

RADIATION EXPOSURE

From 1945 to 1962, the United States conducted numerous nuclear detonation tests: Crossroads (Bikini Atoll); Sandstone, Greenhouse, and Ivy (Eniwetok Atoll); Castle (Bikini Atoll); Pacific Ocean 400 miles southwest of San Diego; Redwing and Hardtack I (Eniwetok and Bikini Atolls); Argus (South Atlantic); and Dominic (Christmas Island, Johnston Island, 400 miles west of San Diego). The main goal was to determine damage caused by the bombs; however, as a result, thousands of military personnel and civilians were exposed to radioactive fallout. Similar tests were conducted within the continental United States, including sites in New Mexico and Nevada. Veterans who participated in activities that directly exposed them to radioactive fallout are referred to as "atomic veterans."

In addition to detonation testing, radioactive releases were also intentionally conducted at U.S. nuclear sites in the years following World War II. According to the U.S. General Accounting Office (GAO), at least 12 planned radioactive releases occurred at three U.S. nuclear sites during 1948-1952. These tests were conducted at Oak Ridge, TN; Dugway, UT; and Los Alamos, NM. Additionally, a planned release occurred at Hanford, WA, in December 1949, which has been referred to as the Green Run test. It is not known how many civilians and military personnel were exposed to fallout from these tests.

In January 1994, the Clinton administration established a Human Radiation Interagency Working Group to coordinate a government-wide effort to uncover the nature and extent of any government-sponsored experiments on individuals involving intentional exposure to ionizing radiation. The working group represents the Administration's response to Secretary of Energy Hazel O'Leary's promise to comb government files for information on hundreds of experiments conducted on people in the 1940s and 1950s.

HALLUCINOGENS

Working with the CIA, the Department of Defense gave hallucinogenic drugs to thousands of "volunteer" soldiers in the 1950s and 1960s. In addition to LSD, the Army also tested quinuclidinyl benzilate, a hallucinogen code-named BZ. Many of these tests were conducted under the so-called MKULTRA program, established to counter perceived Soviet and Chinese advances in brainwashing techniques. Between 1953 and 1964, the program consisted of 149 projects involving drug testing and other studies on unwitting human subjects.

INVESTIGATIONAL DRUGS USED IN THE PERSIAN GULF WAR

Under the Food, Drug, and Cosmetics Act, all vaccines and medical products must be proven safe and effective by the Food and Drug Administration (FDA) in order to be sold and distributed in the United States. This law also applies to medical products used by the Department of Defense, even if given to U.S. troops who are stationed in other countries.

Under current law, an unapproved vaccine or investigational use of a drug could only be administered by the DOD under an Investigational New Drug (IND) procedure. Under an IND, any individual who is given the investigational product must give informed consent, i.e., must be told of the potential risks and benefits of the product, orally and in writing, and choose freely whether or not to participate. In addition, the IND requires that the medical product be distributed under carefully controlled conditions where safety and effectiveness can be evaluated.

When the Department of Defense began preparations for Desert Shield and Desert Storm in 1990, officials were extremely concerned that Iraq would use chemical and biological weapons against the United States. Despite years of study and billions of dollars, the DOD lacked drugs and vaccines that were proven safe and effective to safeguard against anticipated chemical nerve agents and biological toxins. Therefore, DOD officials wanted to use a medication (pyridostigmine bromide) and vaccine (botulinum toxoid) that they believed might protect against chemical nerve agents and botulism. Because the safety and effectiveness of pyridostigmine bromide and botulinum toxoid had not been proven for their intended use, these products were considered investigational drugs.

WARTIME DEMANDS A SEPARATE STANDARD

Edward Martin

Edward Martin, M.D., made this statement, as the Acting Principal Assistant Secretary of Defense in Health Affairs.

■ **POINTS TO CONSIDER**

1. Contrast the mustard gas and lewisite tests with the use of investigational drugs in the Persian Gulf War.

2. Explain why clinical tests of drugs to protect troops against chemical or biological warfare are difficult.

3. According to the military, when is informed consent appropriate?

4. What are the exceptions to the rule of informed consent?

Excerpted from the testimony of Edward Martin, M.D., before the Senate Committee on Veterans' Affairs, May 6, 1994.

During the existence of military combat, military personnel may be exposed to chemical and biological warfare agents. In situations of this kind, informed consent procedures do not in our view apply.

I would like to discuss the use of investigational drugs and biologics and the procedures we have in place which protect the health and welfare of our military personnel when such investigational products are used, both in peacetime and during military combat. Before I address that issue, however, I would like to draw a very clear distinction between the use of such products during the Persian Gulf War, and the human experiments involving mustard agents or lewisite which were conducted almost half a century ago.

RESEARCH VERSUS TREATMENT

Human experiments involving mustard agents or lewisite were conducted during World War II to ascertain the physiological effects of these compounds, to explore potential treatments, and to develop new measures of protection. The intention of these experiments was clearly research; to gain scientific information which was lacking on the effects of exposure to these chemical warfare agents. In addition, this research was conducted prior to any federal policy or regulation for protecting human research subjects. On the other hand, investigational products were employed during the Persian Gulf War as prophylactic treatments against biological and chemical warfare agents. This was not research but direct prevention and treatment.

"INVESTIGATIONAL DRUGS"

Referring to these products as "investigational" is in accordance with Food and Drug Administration (FDA) regulations and not a definitive statement regarding the scientific information available about the products. In the vernacular of the FDA, a drug is "investigational" if it has not been approved by FDA for general commercial marketing for a particularly stated medical purpose. In the Persian Gulf War, the Department of Defense (DOD) used two drugs that, although not approved by FDA for general commercial marketing for the particular medical purposes involved, were specifically allowed by FDA for the special military uses proposed by DOD. FDA allowed these uses because there was evidence they would be effective and no recognized alternative existed, and because FDA thought the use would be safe. The FDA also specifically allowed the use of these drugs in the military combat circumstances involved without the usual informed consent requirements required for investigational products. Withholding the use of these products would have been contrary to the best interests and possibly the lives of our military personnel.

THE PROTOCOL

I would now like to discuss the procedures which protect the health and welfare of our military personnel when investigational products are used, either in peacetime or during military combat.

Studies of new drug or vaccine products are conducted in animals to define dosages that may be safe and effective in humans. The findings from these studies are subsequently reviewed by the FDA as part of an Investigational New Drug (IND) application. Acceptance of the IND by the FDA then permits investigational products to be studied in humans. Under an IND, Phase I trials are conducted in humans to determine the safety of dosage and frequency of administration. Phase II trials are then conducted on a small "at-risk" population to demonstrate the efficacy of the drug or vaccine before application is made to the FDA to begin large scale Phase III trials, which would lead to approval. Approval by the FDA is based upon the results of well designed studies in humans which demonstrate efficacy and safety of the product.

For products designed to protect against biological or chemical warfare agents, a clear demonstration of efficacy would require deliberate exposure of humans to these highly lethal agents in order to determine effectiveness. Such a protocol is clearly unethical in most cases and inappropriate. Thus, in the case of new products designed to protect or treat our troops against lethal biological or chemical warfare agents, the "normal" process of new drug approval is not feasible.

PEACETIME AND WAR

Under the Federal Food, Drug and Cosmetic Act, any use of an IND, whether for research purposes or for treatment purposes, must be preceded by obtaining informed consent from the subject or patient, unless it is "not feasible." In all peacetime military applications, we believe strongly in informed consent and its ethical foundations. Furthermore, in peacetime, we readily agree to inform military personnel, as provided in FDAs regulations, that research is involved, that there may be risks or discomforts, that participation is voluntary and that one may refuse to participate without prejudice. However, during the existence of military combat, military personnel may be exposed to endemic diseases as well as chemical and biological warfare agents in a specified theater of operations. For some of these risks, the best preventive or therapeutic treatment calls for the use of products under IND protocols of the FDA. In situations of this kind, which the FDA interim regulations refer to as "a military combat exigency," informed consent procedures do not in our view apply. However, military personnel are to be given information concerning potential benefits or risks in taking the drugs. In such special circumstances, the FDA Commissioner may approve a DOD request to waive normal informed consent procedures.

THE DRUGS IN QUESTION

During the Persian Gulf War, two IND products, botulinum toxoid and pyridostigmine, were used to protect U.S. personnel against the potential use of biological and chemical warfare agents suspected to be in the Iraqi arsenal. Pyridostigmine is a drug approved by the FDA since 1955 for use in the treatment of myasthenia gravis (MG), a neuromuscular disease. Pyridostigmine has been used safely in the treatment of MG at average daily doses of 600 mg. Pyridostigmine is also regarded as the product of choice by the Armies of the National Atlantic Treaty Organization (NATO) for the pre-treatment of organophosphate nerve agent intoxication and has been held in reserve by the DOD for that use since 1986. The dose used as a pre-treatment in our military personnel during the Persian Gulf War was 15 percent of the average daily dose for MG (30 mg every 8 hrs - i.e., 90 mg daily).

Prior to its use in the Persian Gulf War, botulinum toxoid had been used for more than 20 years in over 3000 individuals with over 10,000 vaccinations to prevent botulism. The use of botulinum toxoid is sponsored by the Centers for Disease Control (CDC) in an IND to make this product available for medical use in persons at risk for occupational exposure to botulism. The FDA has reviewed the annual reports of the administration of botulinum toxoid to at-risk laboratory personnel and it continues to be used safely to protect laboratory workers.

CLASSIFIED INFORMATION

Following the Persian Gulf War, the Assistant Secretary of Defense (Health Affairs) issued a policy memorandum which directed the Military Departments to document in the individual Service member's immunization record and health record information regarding the receipt of anthrax vaccine (a licensed vaccine) or botulinum toxoid. The memorandum also required the Services to retain records regarding distribution of pyridostigmine issued to various combat units. This information was considered classified due to order of battle and deployment of selected force units. The actual use of pyridostigmine was accomplished by individual Service members themselves, and entry into medical records was not possible, since date, time frequency of use and dosage could not be clearly established.

CONCLUSION

In summary, pyridostigmine and botulinum toxoid were not used for experimental purposes in the Persian Gulf War, and the military personnel who received these products were not experimental subjects. These products were used only after careful review both by a duly constituted human use review committee and the FDA. These products were used under the auspices of a treatment protocol, not an experimental protocol. With respect to both drugs, Dr. David Kessler, Commissioner of Food and Drugs, specifically found that in view of the risks associated with the potential use of biological or chemical warfare agents by Iraq and the lack of any alternative therapy, withholding these drugs "would be contrary to the best interests of military personnel."

The Department of Defense is committed to providing our military personnel with safe and effective medical products in peacetime and in combat. Regardless of the scenario, we will continue to furnish medical products to our Service men and women that will meet and respond to the world's evolving military requirements and biomedical technologies.

READING

12

MILITARY PERSONNEL DESERVE NO EXCEPTIONS

Arthur L. Caplan

Arthur Caplan, Ph.D., has worked in the field of medical ethics for more than eighteen years. He is currently Trustee Professor of Bioethics and Director of the Center for Bioethics at the University of Pennsylvania.

■ POINTS TO CONSIDER

1. Describe the difference between military and general research guidelines involving human subjects, according to Caplan.

2. Evaluate the military's claim that the use of investigational drugs during the Persian Gulf War was not research. How does Caplan respond?

3. Discuss the specific concerns about the use of the Gulf War drugs mentioned.

4. Summarize the minimum required of the military in the event that full informed consent is not possible or does not occur.

Excerpted from the prepared statement of Arthur Caplan before the Senate Committee on Veterans' Affairs, April 27, 1994.

Nor does the fact that those who use unproven, untested or unlicensed agents do so with the intent to benefit, treat or prevent harm, transform what is experimental, innovative or research into therapy.

The clash of important values and goals – the importance of achieving the mission set for the military for our nation's well being and the need to protect our troops in order to allow them to accomplish their mission with minimal loss of life and morbidity must be weighed against the need to respect the rights of our fellow citizens who serve in the military. Every American must take responsibility for those who have been injured or made ill as a result of that service. And our government must be vigilant in its efforts to insure that a proper and accountable balance is achieved among these various moral goals.

ETHICS AND WAR

Some would argue that the entire category of ethically suspect research makes no sense in the context of war, hot or cold. When the threat to the nation's security is immediate, real and serious then the prevailing rules of human experimentation requiring the informed consent of subjects and prior review by research review committees must, of necessity, go out the window. The niceties of ethics regarding how to conduct human experimentation are for times of peace, not for the exigencies imposed by the threat or reality of war. But this argument is wrong.

The prevailing standards for human experimentation were set down as a direct response to experiments conducted under conditions of war. The Nuremberg trials at the end of the Second World War promulgated a code of research ethics that has been absorbed into both professional ethics and law by many bodies and governments in the years since that war. The Nuremberg Code makes no exception for research conducted in the context of war. The enormously important goal of protecting the nation's security is not held to be a value that is so overriding as to obliterate the individual subject's rights. The Code states clearly and unambiguously that everyone involved in research is to be so informed and that they are to have the right to give or withhold their consent to that research.

SAME MORAL STANDARDS

The need for informed consent and peer review of proposed research as essential prerequisites to justify experimentation is not changed by the existence of a state of war. Moral standards have not shifted concerning the requirement for informed consent at any time during the past fifty years. Our own current law governing the use of human subjects where funding for research comes from the Department of Defense is not ambiguous:

"Funds...may not be used for research...unless the informed consent of the subject is obtained in advance..." (P.L. 98-525, 1401 (c), October 19, 1984, 98 Stat. 2615.)

What can be debated and what is more appropriate to debate is whether every untested and unproven medical intervention undertaken in the context of impending conflict or war constitutes research. What can and should be debated is the degree to which circumstances and conditions conspire to make the application of standing moral principles governing research practical or impractical at times when war is imminent or has actually been declared.

WHAT IS RESEARCH?

If a goal of undertaking an intervention with a human being is to generate new knowledge then that activity counts as research. Some forms of intervention carried out by our military or security agencies indisputably fall into the category of research. When persons are subjected to high doses of radiation, when they are given LSD or other agents, when persons are asked to subject themselves to exposure to toxic agents in order to understand the impact of these agents on the human body, the intent of such actions is clearly research.

But, the label of research does not always clearly apply to actions taken in war. For example, during the War in the Gulf, a number of actions were considered and taken to try and protect military personnel against the perceived risk of biological or chemical weapons attack.

GULF WAR DRUGS

Pyridostigmine bromide tablets were given to more than two thirds of the troops in the field, about four hundred thousand soldiers. These tablets were given in the hope that they might pro-

Source: Hearing before the U.S. Senate Committee on Veterans' Affairs, August 5, 1994.

vide protection against the use of nerve gas. The tablets have never been approved to use for this purpose.

Consideration was also given during Operation Desert Shield to the mass administration of botulinum pentavalent toxoid via vaccination. This vaccine, while used by more than 3,000 persons during the 1970s who worked in laboratories where exposure to botulism bacteria was possible, had also not been approved. No systematic data on safety and efficacy for this vaccine has ever been collected. Still, when the request was made for approval to waive informed consent for the use of this vaccine to the Food and Drug Administration and the Department of Defense "informed consent waiver group," it was granted. Ultimately, it appears that as many as 8,000 troops were given one or two shots of botulinum pentavalent toxoid.

THE ARGUMENT

It may well be argued that the use of these agents to protect those involved in military operations against attack from chemical or biological weapons is not research. Indeed, that seems to have been the thinking of many of those involved in the decision to grant a waiver from standing informed consent requirements for the use of botulinum pentavalent toxoid and anti-nerve gas tablets. There had been previous use of these agents in human beings. There were some reports in the medical literature about these agents. And, most importantly, the reason and intent behind administering these agents was to protect troops in order to minimize casualties and permit the performance of the military mission assigned to these forces by the President.

But, these arguments against the appropriateness of applying the label "research" to the use of these agents during Desert Shield are not persuasive. The use of unapproved, unlicensed agents clearly was understood by the Food and Drug Administration (FDA) and the Department of Defense (DOD) to be research in as much as both agencies recognized the need to seek waivers from prevailing informed consent requirements. And regulatory and military officials understood that the very reasons why practical circumstances made it difficult to obtain consent for the use of untested, unproven agents in large populations deployed in trying environments under battlefield conditions meant that the use of these agents had to be seen as experimental.

MOTIVES DON'T CHANGE REALITY

It can be argued that those who sought to use agents that might confer a prophylactic benefit on American military personnel did so by weighing carefully the cost, risk and potential benefits to be obtained. But, the fact that careful weighing of risk and benefit comes out in favor of using untested, unproven and unlicensed agents in the hope of securing a benefit does not transform an experimental intervention into a therapy. Nor does the fact that those who use unproven, untested or unlicensed agents do so with the intent to benefit, treat or prevent harm, transform what is experimental, innovative or research into therapy. If that were so then those who do research would merely have to change their intentions and they could succeed in making the most innovative and experimental medical interventions into therapies merely by a change of mind.

The regulatory definition of research, intent to create generalizable knowledge, is sound as far as it goes. But, it does not go far enough. For what is needed is a term that can capture activities that are manifestly experimental but are not conducted with the intent of generating new knowledge.

GULF WAR EXPOSURES

During their deployment associated with the Persian Gulf War, many of the approximately 700,000 veterans of the Gulf War may have been exposed to a variety of potentially hazardous substances. These substances include compounds used to decontaminate equipment and protect it against chemical agents, fuel used as a sand suppressant in and around encampments, fuel oil used to burn human waste, fuel in shower water, leaded vehicle exhaust used to dry sleeping bags, depleted uranium, parasites, pesticides, drugs to protect against chemical warfare agents (such as pyridostigmine bromide), and smoke from oil well fires. Moreover, DOD acknowledged in June 1996 that some veterans may have been exposed to the nerve agent sarin following the post-war demolition of Iraqi ammunition facilities.

Donna Heivilin, "Gulf War Illness," **Government Accounting Office**, June 25, 1997: 2.

UNCERTAIN OUTCOMES

This is obviously what took place in the Gulf with anti-botulism toxoid and pyridostigmine. These agents were used in large populations for purposes other than those for which they were originally designed in circumstances under which they had never before been tried. Moreover, in the case of both agents it was not clear exactly what chemical or biological agents might have put into the field by our adversary. This meant that the agents used may have had no efficacy or might actually have had an adverse effect in the case of the utilization of certain nerve gas agents. The circumstances which prevailed in the combat environment of the Gulf also meant that these agents were administered in a manner that deviated a great deal from the previous use of these agents such as when troops were given only one or two shots of anti-botulism toxoid when three shots were believed to be essential in order to achieve efficacy.

The case for considering the use of unapproved and unlicensed agents in dire circumstances as manifestly falling into the research end of the research to therapy spectrum is further cemented by the obvious uncertainty that accompanied the utilization of these agents as to the efficacy they would have in the field. In reviewing the documents that led to the decision to grant waivers of informed consent for the utilization of these anti-biological and anti-chemical warfare agents, it seems plain that the most accurate description that can be given for the decision to grant the waiver is that there was a chance the agents would do more good than harm but that the efficacy of these agents to prevent harm was seen as far from certain.

IF NOT CONSENT...

When research is done in situations where, for a variety of reasons, full informed consent is not possible, researchers will at least strive to let individuals know that they are involved in an investigational, innovative or research activity. These would appear to be a requirement even in conditions of impending or actual war.

In the context of the Persian Gulf War, medical follow-up for those exposed to anti-biological and anti-chemical warfare agents seems to have been at most, minimal. Not only is this duty owed to those exposed in terms of establishing whether harm or injury has occurred, but it is also morally incumbent upon those who waive standing ethical protections for research to compile as much information as possible about the benefits and risks associated with the use of new agents, so that this information can then be brought to bear in future situations where military personnel are facing the prospect of chemical or biological warfare.

READING

13

THREE SOLDIERS

Rudolph R. Mills
Earl P. Davenport
Neil R. Tetzlaff

Rudolph R. Mills served in the U.S. Navy from December 1944 - July 1946. Earl P. Davenport served in the U.S. Army from December 1958 - June 1960. He then served in a civilian position at the Dugway Proving Ground, Utah. Neil R. Tetzlaff is a retired lieutenant colonel in the U.S. Air Force. He is a Gulf War Veteran.

■ **POINTS TO CONSIDER**

1. Discuss the type of duties the three men performed for the military.

2. Why is Mills revealing his story fifty years later?

3. How does Tetzlaff link pyridostigmine to his sickness?

4. What does Davenport believe specifically led to his illness?

Excerpted from the prepared statements of Rudolph R. Mills, Earl P. Davenport, and Neil R. Tetzlaff before the Senate Veterans' Affairs Committee, May 6, 1994.

STATEMENT OF RUDOLPH R. MILLS

I was among those who received high doses of mustard gas.

Fifty years ago, in December 1944, my twin brother and I quit high school to join the U.S. Navy. World War II was still going on and we wanted to serve our country. Once we were inducted we went our separate ways. I was at Recruit Training in Bainbridge, Maryland, when a call came for volunteers to participate in gas mask experiments. I stepped forward. I was seventeen years old, just out of boot camp and willing to do anything to help my country. And it wasn't just me, there were thousands of patriotic young Americans who felt the same.

In April of 1945 I participated in gas chamber experiments with the same gas mask approximately a dozen times for an hour each time. I had on an experimental mask and the Navy was trying to determine if people wearing these masks could communicate with each other. I was enticed to sing over the intercom. At the time I could sing quite well. I remember the corpsman conducting the tests seemed serious about "taking me uptown" for tryouts. When I sang, the air pressure of my voice caused the sides of the mask to open up and I suffered burns on my cheeks and chin. No one ever told me that the mask became less effective against the gas with each use.

We were sworn to secrecy and it wasn't until 45 years later that I learned I had been part of around 4,000 or more servicemen who were human guinea pigs in gas experiments conducted from 1942 through 1945 by the Chemical Warfare Service. I was among those who received high doses of mustard gas.

Even before my discharge in July 1946, my health started to deteriorate. I started to lose my teeth and I had a chronic sore throat. Within three years of my discharge my tonsils and all teeth had to be removed. I developed a hacking cough when I was in my twenties which culminated in a diagnosis of cancer of the larynx in 1970. At the age of 43 I underwent a long series of radiation treatments and later surgery to remove part of my voice box and larynx. This left me with difficulty breathing, and the voice you hear today.

STATEMENT OF EARL P. DAVENPORT

I never doubted the assurances and judgments of my superiors.

I entered the Army in 1956. I was stationed at Dugway (Dugway Proving Ground in Nevada) in December of 1958 through June of 1960 where I worked as a clerk who delivered supplies to support toxic field test areas. In 1960, I was discharged from active duty. In 1962, I went to work at Dugway as a civilian in the position of a decontamination equipment operator. I worked with a variety of agents; VX, GD, GB, BZ, mustard gas, tear gas, and nerve gas simulants. I also worked with a variety of biological agents; U, X, UL, etc.

Both biological and chemical tests were conducted in the open air by many delivery systems. This required military and civilian personnel to wear protective clothing and also take biological shots. We were told they were to build up our immunity to the agents we were testing. We were never told the names of these shots; we were only given the symbols. When I questioned taking these shots, I was told I was receiving hazard pay and it was part of my job. At this time hazard pay was six cents an hour.

Like many workers at Dugway, I never doubted the assurances and judgments of my superiors, who briefed me on the hazards of my job. But, I assumed, that if they were wrong, the government would take responsibility for it and protect its workers. Now I am wondering if I was wrong.

On July 13 of 1984, I was involved in a test the Army was conducting to test a laser system that would detect nerve agents. I was operating a sprayer, blowing a fog of nerve agent simulant called DMMP (dimethyl methylphosphonate) into the path of a laser beam. During the test I noticed a sudden shift in the wind direction and quickly cut off the sprayer. But, before I could don my protective mask, a cloud of the chemical covered me. I could feel it on my skin and taste it; it was oily. I tried to wipe it off as best I could and put my mask on. I secured my area, then left the test site to shower. At that time I was checked out by a medic and seemed to be OK. I then reported to my supervisor to fill out an accident report. I was told at that time if I became ill to report to the base hospital.

I wasn't too concerned about getting hit with a simulant. I trusted the Army's assurance that DMMP was "practically non-toxic" according to the material safety data sheets [MSDS] that were available to the employees at the time of the test. It also stated that DMMP may irritate the mucous membranes and respiratory tract, and that prolonged skin contact may cause irritation, blisters and burns. Dugway's Safety Office recommends workers wear a military protective mask, rubber gloves and apron.

The day after the accident I felt different. I was wheezing and coughing up phlegm. After two weeks my condition had not improved so I went to the Dugway Army Hospital. I was given cough syrup and antibiotics for what they diagnosed as bronchitis, but after several weeks there was still no improvement in my condition, so I was sent to the University of Utah for further evaluation. There I was diagnosed as having a mild exacerbation of chronic obstructive pulmonary disease by irritant effect of DMMP.

Over the years my condition worsened. I seemed to get colds and bronchitis more frequently and was short of breath, especially at high altitudes. In 1988, I suffered a heart attack and by 1992, I missed an average of six days of work a month due to illness. Twice I left work in an ambulance because of heart and breathing problems. The days I seemed to feel the worst were when outdoor simulant tests were conducted. At this time, because of medications I needed to take for my heart and lung problems, I was considered a safety risk and was eventually removed from chemical and bio-agent work. In 1993, at the urging of my doctors, I took an early retirement.

I was very concerned about my health and the connection to the DMMP exposure, especially with my past history of working with chemical and biological agents and the possibility of unknown and low-level exposures. Also there were the shots I had been given.

I did some research and found that the Government had underestimated the health hazards of DMMP. Dugway safety officials confirmed that DMMP was used extensively as a simulant for chemical agents until 1988, when the Army Surgeon General reviewed studies identifying it as a "suspect carcinogen." Although the Army clearly miscalculated the health hazards of DMMP for several years, the government concluded my health problems were caused because I smoked and not because of my exposure to DMMP.

STATEMENT OF NEIL R. TETZLAFF, LT. COL., USAF (RET.)

During the nuclear tests in the 40s, radiation wasn't considered hazardous, and during Vietnam, agent orange wasn't considered harmful. Pyridostigmine, taken at the dose of 30mg every eight hours, is considered to be noninjurious to humans by the Department of Defense (DOD).

In August of 1990 I was a Lieutenant Colonel in the USAF serving as the Assistant Deputy Commander for Resource Management for the 48th Tactical Fighter Wing, RAF Lakenheath, United Kingdom. On the 20th of August, with six hours notice, I was deployed with 11 others as the advance party pursuant to the deployment of the 48th's F-111s to Saudi Arabia.

While being mobilized I was issued a seven-day supply of pyridostigmine bromide pills and was told to start taking them on an eight-hour schedule, which I did. The package contained no warnings. For me this was a chronic overdose of pyridostigmine. Both my immediate physical and mental symptoms corroborate this fact.

On the plane ride to Saudi, and during my first day in-country, I was nauseated and vomited. I attributed the sickness to the plane ride and tenseness of the situation. On my second day there I vomited again and felt "different"; I attributed the sickness to something I'd eaten. On the third day I was extremely nauseated and vomited many times. I sought out the doctor and discussed my illness with him. We dismissed it as something I had eaten at the Saudi canteen. On my fourth day there I vomited violently, the worst ever of my life, and was acting a bit off center and muddled. On the fifth day I didn't vomit but was sore, lost much of my bounce, acted strangely silly and was totally out of character. On the sixth day I was incoherent, extremely tired, and at times irrational. On the morning of the seventh day I vomited about a quart of blood.

I knew then I was in deep trouble and I headed straight for the doctor. Shortly thereafter, I began to lose consciousness, and the doctor started an I.V. After examining me in the Tiaf clinic, the doctor commandeered a C-130 and air-evacuated me to the Royal Saudi Hospital in Riyadh. The plane ride to Riyadh was extremely painful; every bump sent pain throughout my body. Though the worst of the pain was in my abdomen, my back, neck, head, arms, and legs were also in pain.

At the hospital, I was given a general anesthetic to knock me out. Doctors looked in my stomach and found a tear of approximately one and three quarters inches. They fed me intravenously for two days, put me on a special diet, and then released me to USAF medical personnel after a total of four days in the hospital.

Since taking pyridostigmine while deployed for Desert Shield, I have been suffering moderate, severe, and intolerable pain, fatigue easily and lately have developed one heck of a palsy. I've lost my ability to speak because I can't recall words. The last three and a half years have been extremely difficult on my family and me. This brief description by no means enumerates the mental and physical disabilities I've had to overcome.

As the situation stands now, the disabling effects of pyridostigmine are not known and are not being investigated (by the DOD or Veterans Administration), even though the drug was used during Desert Storm on an experimental basis. I am caught in the same dilemma as the victims of Crossroads and agent orange. During the nuclear tests in the 40s, radiation wasn't considered hazardous; and during Vietnam, agent orange wasn't considered harmful. Pyridostigmine, taken at the dose of 30mg every eight hours, is considered to be noninjurous to humans by the DOD.

RECOGNIZING AUTHOR'S POINT OF VIEW

This activity may be used as an individualized study guide for students in libraries and resource centers or as a discussion catalyst in small group and classroom discussions.

Many readers are unaware that written material usually expresses an opinion or bias. The capacity to recognize an author's point of view is an essential reding skill. The skill to read with insight and understanding involves the ability to detect different kinds of opinions or bias. **Sex bias, race bias, ethnocentric bias, political bias** and **religious bias** are five basic kinds of opinions expressed in editorials and all literature that attempts to persuade. They are briefly defined in the glossary below.

Five Kinds of Editorial Opinion or Bias

Sex Bias — The expression of dislike for and/or feeling of superiority over the opposite sex or a particular sexual minority.

Race Bias — The expression of dislike for and/or feeling of superiority over a racial group.

Ethnocentric Bias — The expression of a belief that one's own group, race, religion, culture, or nation is superior. Ethnocentric persons judge others by their own standards and values.

Political Bias — The expression of political opinions and attitudes about domestic or foreign affiars.

Religious Bias — The expression of a religious belief or attitude.

Guidelines

1. Locate three examples of political opinion or bias in the readings from Chapter Three.

2. Locate five sentences that provide examples of any kind of editorial opinion or bias from the readings in Chapter Three.

3. Write down each of the above sentences and determine what kind of bias each sentence represents. Is it sex bias, race bias, ethnocentric bias, political bias or religious bias?

4. Make up one-sentence statements that would be an example of each of the following: sex bias, race bias, ethnocentric bias, political bias and religious bias.

5. See if you can locate five sentences that are factual statements from the readings in Chapter Three.

Summarize the author's point of view in one sentence for each of the following readings:

Reading 6 _____

_____

Reading 7 _____

_____

Reading 8 _____

_____

Reading 9 _____

_____

Reading 10 _____

_____

Reading 11 _____

_____

CHAPTER 4

HUMAN RADIATION EXPERIMENTS

READING

14

THIRTY YEARS OF HUMAN RADIATION EXPERIMENTS IN THE UNITED STATES

Department of Energy

Preceded by the Manhattan Project, the Atomic Energy Commission and the Energy Research and Development Administration, the Department of Energy released its report in February 1995 on the thirty-year legacy of human radiation experiments sponsored by it and its predecessors. Included on its list are 435 documented experiments from WWII to the mid-1970s, including an estimated 16,000 subjects. Public knowledge of the experiments came as early as 1976. Ten years later, the Markey report, released by a congressional committee, criticized 30 government sponsored human radiation experiments and the plutonium injections. In December 1993, Secretary of Energy Hazel O'Leary announced that the Department was to reveal the scope and scale of human radiation experiments sponsored by the Department of Energy (DOE).

■ POINTS TO CONSIDER

1. Describe the evolution of atomic/nuclear research from the DOE standpoint.

2. Evaluate the justification for plutonium experiments with humans. Discuss the controversy associated with these experiments.

3. Summarize the scale and scope of environmental radiation releases.

4. Why are the experiments conducted by DOE and its predecessors in question today?

Human Radiation Experiments: The Department of Energy Roadmap to the Story and the Records, U.S. Department of Energy, February 1995. Available to the public from the U.S. Department of Commerce, Technology Administration and the National Technical Information Service, Springfield, VA 22161, (703) 487-4650.

Until the war, biomedical researchers at these universities had used radiation as a tool to study biological systems and disease. The Manhattan Project shifted this research to study the metabolism and health effects of radiation itself.

On April 10, 1945, medical staff of the U.S. Manhattan Engineer District in Oak Ridge, TN, injected plutonium into the victim of a car accident. American scientists had only recently begun producing plutonium, and thousands of workers were laboring to produce the quantities required for the first atomic bombs. While aware that plutonium was hazardous, project officials were uncertain how much exposure would cause harm. Desire for information about human metabolism and retention of plutonium led to this first injection in Oak Ridge. Over the next two years, 17 other people also received plutonium injections.

THE DOE PROJECT

The Manhattan Project and its postwar successor, the U.S. Atomic Energy Commission (AEC), also carried out human experiments with uranium, polonium, americium, and other radioactive substances. Radiation tests continued after the War; some of these studies took place under AEC supervision and had direct defense-related applications. The agency also sponsored substantial programs in the medical applications of radiation and in basic biomedical research. In addition, independent physicians and researchers at universities and hospitals conducted many post-war human radiation studies to develop the techniques of present-day nuclear medicine.

The role of the U.S. Government in conducting or sponsoring human radiation experiments has become the subject of public debate. Questions have been raised about the purpose, extent, and health consequences of these studies, and about how subjects were selected. The extent to which subjects provided informed consent is also under scrutiny. To respond to these questions, the Clinton Administration directed the U.S. Department of Energy (DOE), along with other Federal agencies, to retrieve and inventory all records that document human radiation experiments. Many such records are now publicly available and will permit an open accounting and understanding of what took place.

Human radiation experiments encompass many additional

topics beyond those presented here. Yet the three that are discussed are of particular relevance to DOE, and sufficient information is available about them to tell a meaningful story.

WORLD WAR II AND THE MANHATTAN PROJECT

Early in 1942, officials of the Manhattan Project realized they needed a special medical program associated with the secret project to build an atomic bomb. Work was underway to construct mammoth industrial facilities to produce plutonium and uranium-235, key bomb materials.

Until the war, biomedical researchers at these universities had used radiation as a tool to study biological systems and disease. The Manhattan Project shifted this research to study the metabolism and health effects of radiation itself. For example, experiments at Rochester included studies of chronic low levels of radiation and development of improved detection instruments.

Inhalation, ingestion, and injection of radioactive materials were studied at all three universities under Manhattan Project contracts. Most of these studies involved animals, and their chief purpose was to determine where in the body these materials collected and at what rate the materials were excreted. This information was needed to judge the radiation dose from the material and the estimated corresponding hazard.

While the animal studies provided important data, researchers wanted precise human data to establish firm radiation exposure guidelines. As a result, human studies were authorized. Some researchers used themselves as subjects: six researchers at the Chicago Met Lab drank solutions of plutonium to study excretion rates. Other studies used hospital patients, and included injections of radioactive polonium and uranium in patients at Rochester's Strong Memorial Hospital. Plutonium was also injected into subjects in the Oak Ridge Hospital, the University of Chicago Billings Hospital, the University of California Medical School, and Strong Memorial Hospital. Data from these human experiments and related research were used to set worker exposure standards. These standards, in turn, were used to analyze the various industrial processes to set needs for shielding, ventilation, and other worker-safety measures.

POSTWAR RESEARCH

After the War, there was a great deal of interest in conducting further biomedical research with radiation. This interest correlated with a vastly enhanced knowledge of radioactive materials and the recently developed ability to produce large volumes of radioisotopes in nuclear reactors.

Scientists who had used radiation for metabolic studies or for medical diagnosis and treatment before the War, now envisioned broad new avenues of radiation research. The U.S. Government shared this view, as did the public. Impressed with the remarkable success of the Manhattan Project and awed by the power of the atomic bomb, the nation was receptive to using radioactivity to solve problems. There was also a new willingness for the Government to fund and support research. As a result, the Manhattan Project and later the AEC moved aggressively into civilian biomedical research while continuing defense-related applications.

A disease of major interest to biomedical research was cancer. Cancer was a focal point because it was widespread, and because radiation had shown early promise as a possible treatment and diagnostic tool. Some cancer tumors could be destroyed or greatly reduced by radiation; if effective doses could be delivered to a cancerous spot, patients could be helped.

THE EXPERIMENTS, PART 1

Discovered in 1941 by Glenn Seaborg and others at Berkeley, plutonium supported nuclear fission, a process that split atoms and released tremendous energy. Plutonium became an urgently needed material for one variety of atomic bomb; uranium-235, the fissionable isotope of natural uranium, was used in the other bomb type.

The first appreciable quantities of plutonium became available by January 1944. At that time, Seaborg warned of its potential health hazards and suggested immediate studies to learn its bio-logical behavior. The first human plutonium injection took place on April 10, 1945, at the Oak Ridge Hospital.

How all the injections were coordinated – or even if they were coordinated – is unclear. Following the Oak Ridge test, injections were given at the Billings Hospital at the University of Chicago on

April 26, 1945, and at the University of California Hospital in San Francisco on May 14, 1945. By late June, Manhattan Project contractors at the University of Rochester's Strong Memorial Hospital developed a detailed plan for "rapid (one year) Completion of Human Tracer Studies." These studies were to include plutonium, uranium, polonium, and radioactive lead.

THE EXPERIMENTS, PART 2

The U.S. Government had adopted requirements mandating that subjects give informed consent as a condition of research. Questions arose whether the plutonium subjects provided consent for the original experiments or for the 1973 follow-up examinations. The ensuing investigation resulted in two internal AEC reports issued in August 1974. Both concluded that only one subject may have provided any kind of consent. The other 17 participated with little verifiable knowledge of the experiment or its risks. Moreover, the reports found that the 1973 follow-up studies were also not done with informed consent from the subjects. Three subjects were not told they had been injected with plutonium for experimental purposes, nor why they had been asked to return to the hospital.

Although the AEC did not publicly release reports on these experiments, the agency's successor, the Energy Research and Development Administration, issued a fact sheet on the matter in 1976. This issuance provided details on the experiments and briefly discussed results from the 1974 AEC inquiry on informed consent.

RADIOACTIVE RELEASES, EXPERIMENTS AND THE PUBLIC

The Manhattan Project and its successors investigated various aspects of radiological warfare, which would use radioactive sources to contaminate a targeted area. Nuclear explosions would not be involved. Rather, radioactive material would be placed in a casing for battlefield dispersal. Among the purposes envisioned for these weapons were to injure enemy soldiers, block troop advances, and contaminate enemy cities. Radiological warfare weapons also were conceived as a tool to instill fear in adversaries and to serve as a deterrent to their use against America.

In 1954, the Atomic Energy Act was amended and the AEC given authority to declassify certain areas of nuclear technology to promote commercial nuclear power and international peaceful atomic energy activities. Concurrent with the development of these applications, public concern about the hazards of fallout from atmospheric nuclear weapons testing was increasing. The releases discussed below are closely tied to these concerns and include analysis of fallout effects, reactor safety testing, nuclear rocket and aircraft tests, and plant safety testing. With one exception, these experiments were not classified.

Hanford: 1962 and 1963 releases – In 1962 and 1963, Hanford intentionally released small amounts of iodine-131 to study the dispersion of radioactive iodine into the air and soil.

Idaho National Engineering Laboratory (INEL): Controlled Environmental Radioiodine Tests (CERT) – The CERT activities involved intentional releases of radioiodine to the environment and were intended to evaluate the health hazards of reactor accidents. Twenty-four tests undertaken from 1963 to 1968 were designed to develop models for predicting movement of radioiodine through the air-vegetation-cow-milk-human food chain.

The Kiwi Transient Nuclear Test (TNT), conducted in 1965, simulated a worst case accident occurring during the launch of a nuclear-powered spacecraft. The test involved a controlled nuclear excursion resulting in partial vaporization of the reactor core. This created a radioactive plume that, while low in radioactivity, was detectable far off-site. Los Alamos collected environmental data from the test point to approximately 50 miles downwind. The U.S. Public Health Service monitored the cloud to beyond 200 miles downwind, which extended to Los Angeles and the Pacific Ocean.

Paducah, KY, Gaseous Diffusion Plant: uranium hexafluoride tests – Four deliberate releases of uranium hexafluoride (UF6) were made to the atmosphere at the Paducah Gaseous Diffusion Plant. Two occurred in 1955; the other two took place in 1974. The tests were conducted to study the airborne behavior of UF6. There is no record of human experimentation associated with these tests.

Oak Ridge environmental research areas – The Oak Ridge Health Physics Division established various environmental research areas to evaluate the behavior of radionuclides in the environment. These areas functioned in conjunction with a radioecology program begun in 1954. Laboratory and field studies used 18 different radionuclides to study the uptake, accumulation, and movement of isotopes in terrestrial and aquatic food chains; rates of translocation in plants; consumption of food and turnover of isotopes by terrestrial and aquatic insects and other invertebrates, fish and, mammals; and reentry of isotopes into the soil through fungi, bacteria, and soil animals.

15

THE UNIVERSITY OF CINCINNATI EXPERIMENTS 1961-1972: THE POINT

David S. Egilman

David S. Egilman, M.D., is a physician in Braintree, Massachusetts. He also teaches and researches history of the development of 20th century medical knowledge in his faculty position at Brown University. Egilman spent a decade researching and attempting to publicize his criticism of the human radiation experiments at the University of Cincinnati.

■ POINTS TO CONSIDER

1. Evaluate the author's claim that ethical objections to the UC experiments exist.

2. Describe why the author believes whole body radiation (WBR) is a suspect treatment in these experiments.

3. Discuss other procedures in treatment that the author finds questionable.

4. What does the author believe to have been the purpose of the research?

Excerpted from the testimony of David S. Egilman before the Subcommittee on Administrative Law and Governmental Relations of the House of Representatives Judiciary Committee, April 11, 1994.

If this was therapy and it worked, why did the researchers stop it when it became public? Did the researchers stop the experiments because they became public?

On November 28, 1950, Dr. Joseph Hamilton wrote a letter to Shields Warren, M.D., Director, Division of Biology and Medicine, the Atomic Energy Commission (AEC) concerning the ability of irradiated soldiers to function. AEC researchers wanted to determine the dose that might limit a soldier's "capacity to execute intricate tasks for which physical well being is essential." He discussed the difficulties of performing such a research study, and suggested that "for both politic and scientific reasons,...it would be advantageous to secure what data can be obtained by using large monkeys such as chimpanzees which are somewhat more responsive than lower mammals." If the research was to be done on humans, Dr. Hamilton predicted that "those concerned in the AEC would be subject to considerable criticism, as admittedly this would have a little of the Buchenwald touch...The volunteers should be on a freer basis than inmates of a prison. At this point, I haven't any very constructive ideas as to where one would turn for such volunteers should this plan be put into execution."

Despite Hamilton's "political" sensitivity to a possible adverse public reaction to this research, the Department of Defense (DOD) funded studies similar to those described in his letter. Eugene Saenger, M.D., and his fellow researchers at the University of Cincinnati (UC) conducted these experiments between 1960 and 1971. In all, researchers irradiated 88 cancer patients during those years. Dr. Saenger and coworkers published some of their findings in 1969 in the *Archives of General Psychiatry*. The article was titled, "Total and Half Body Irradiation, Effect on Cognitive and Emotional Processes."

Cancer therapy was not the purpose of this research. Recently some defenders of this work have stated that the experiments met the ethical standard of their day. This is not true.

DEVIL IN THE DETAILS

As they say, the devil is in the details. In their 1969 paper the researchers stated that pre-irradiation analysis of the experimental subjects revealed that the researchers would have had difficulty in obtaining true informed consent from the study participants.

"Relevant intellectual characteristics of the patient sample were as follows: a low-educational level (ranging from 63 to 112 on the full-scale of the Wechsler-Bellevue which has a mean of 84.5), and a strong evidence of cerebral organic deficit in the baseline (pre-radiation) measure of most patients." Thirteen of sixteen subjects were "negro;" three were white.

These researchers like others involved in similar experiments funded by the Department of Energy (DOE) and NASA, selected the most vulnerable of our citizens as subjects, the poor, the mentally and emotionally impaired, and African-Americans. UC researchers knew or should have known that their patient population was incapable of giving informed consent, even if they had been informed of the experimental risks (which they were not). The UC researchers did not give the subjects all the facts on the side effects of the radiation. Therefore, if the patients consented to the experiments, the consent was not informed.

According to the UC investigation of this research (Suskind Report) a review of 27 of 33 patient charts between 1960-1964 did not contain any notation that the patients were informed about anything. Six of the patient charts contained information indicating that the patient "was informed about the nature of the treatment and its possible benefits." The patient charts did not contain any notation on the risks of the experiments. It must be assumed from comments of relatives of survivors and the lack of notation that 27 of 33 patients received little or no information of the risks. The researchers' own contradictory statements about informed consent provide the best evidence that they violated the ethical and moral standards of both the sixties and the nineties.

INFORMED CONSENT

UC researchers in their 1969 research paper revealed these contradictory elements themselves. The report included both of the following statements: "In each case the patient was advised that the therapy might be beneficial to him but that it was experimental in nature. Informed consent was obtained in all cases." And, "There was no discussion with the patient of possible subjective reactions resulting from the treatment. Other physicians, nurses, technicians and ward personnel were instructed not to discuss post-irradiation symptoms or reactions with the patient. This precaution was carefully followed so as to standardize and minimize "iatrogenic" factors in influencing whatever subjective reactions the patients might have to radiation." *Iatrogenic* means doctor-induced. The researchers claim they did not tell the patients about the possible side effects because this information could have induced nausea and vomiting in the patients. This is further evidence that the study was a study of the side effects of radiation, not of the treatment of cancer. It is obviously impossible to obtain informed consent without giving information on the side effects of the treatment.

Having failed to provide informed consent, (how could their patient population possibly give informed consent?) they had to lie about it when the experiments became public. There is no better evidence that they violated their own and our own ethical and moral standards. The researchers were so aware of the importance of informed consent that they stated they received it from the participants in the experiment even though it is clear they did not.

The legal importance of informed consent was established in 1914, when Justice Cardozo wrote that, "every human being...has a right to determine what shall be done with his own body, and a surgeon who performs an operation without his patient's consent commits an assault for which he is liable in damages." Schloendorf v. Society of New York Hospital, 211 NY 125 (1914).

WHOLE BODY IRRADIATION

Researchers tested the efficacy of whole body irradiation (WBR) in the 1930s-50s at several centers, including Memorial-Sloan Kettering in New York City. WBR was not useful in the treatment of solid tumors. Researchers found that the so-called "non-radiosensitive cancers" such as those that UC researcher irradiated were unresponsive to whole body radiotherapy. The medical utility of this study was suspect and disguised, and as a result the research resulted in the deaths of at least eight, and probably more than twenty of the participants.

In a separate article titled "Whole Body Radiotherapy of Advanced Cancer," Dr. Saenger, et al., wrote, "If one assumes that all severe drops of blood cell count and all instances of hypocellular or acellular marrow at death were due only to radiation and not influenced by previous therapy, then one can identify eight cases in which there is a possibility of the therapy contributing to mortality." Suskind states that up to 19 may have died as a result of the radiation.

In 1905, Dessauer first used irradiation of the entire body for purposes of the experimental therapy of disease. Physicians used whole body irradiation for treatment of a wide variety of benign conditions including asthma, migraine, and arthritis. Reports of adverse effects from radiation quickly narrowed the use of the treatment to metastatic tumors.

Physicians conducted a set of clinical trials of whole body irradiation for cancer at Memorial-Sloan Kettering in New York from 1931 through the 1940s. Physicians published progress reports of the experiments performed at Memorial in 1932, 1934, and 1942. The reports were in agreement with other literature from that time. The technique of whole body irradiation showed some promise with leukemias and lymphomas, but "little or no benefit follows its use in the treatment of generalized carcinoma or sarcoma." (Medinger and Craver, 1942). In the same study, Medinger and Craver explained why the therapy did not work on carcinomas (the type of cancer selected for the UC experiments): "The results in these generalized carcinoma cases were discouraging. The reason for this is quickly apparent. Carcinomas are much more radioresistant than lymphomatoid tumors, and by total body irradiation the dose cannot be nearly large enough to alter these tumors appreciably." The reason the dose cannot be large enough

DIRTY MEDICINE?

Recently revealed records show that 61 African Americans were guinea pigs along with 12 others in a 12-year military study at the University of Cincinnati Medical Center designed to see how exposure to full- and partial-body radiation 10 times higher than normal would affect the body. After 60 days of exposure to the radiation (250 rads in one session), 25 of the patients died.

The tests were conducted from 1960 to 1972 by Eugene L. Saenger, an eminent radiological health specialist. Saenger knew something was wrong as he wrote a report to the Defense Department stating, "one can identify eight cases in which there is a possibility of the therapy contributing to mortality." Ironically, Saenger also serves as a key governmental witness on radiation lawsuit cases brought against the Department of Energy.

Dr. David S. Egilman has been researching the Cincinnati experiments for over ten years and did not mince words when he told us, "What they did was murder those black patients. And those researchers, Gottschalk and Saenger, are as dirty as Mengele."

Anthony and Denise Ji-Ahnte Sibert, "Medical Repression," **Z Magazine**, May 1994: 17-18.

is that a dose that will kill the tumor will also kill the patient. Later studies found similar results.

QUESTIONABLE PURPOSE

Interestingly Dr. Aron, one of the UC researchers and a member of the UC committee that investigated the appropriateness of this work in the early 1970s, recently stated, "In Cincinnati, the patients' disease had spread throughout their bodies, and most were given a life expectancy of six months. The effect of the study was a short prolongation of their lives. All who had the treatment have died of their cancers. They lived an average of fifteen months after the radiation exposure." If this was therapy and it worked, why did the researchers stop it when it became public?

Did the researchers stop the experiments because they became public? If the radiation did not help, the subjects, who lived an average of 15 months after being irradiated, were not really suffering from terminal cancer. They were not. The researchers reported that until they were irradiated, most of the patients were in "relatively good health." Suskind's report indicated that the researchers excluded terminal patients from the study; "Some of the reasons for patient rejection included advanced state of malignancies leading to disorientation, stupor, and/or coma, and terminal advanced malignant disease in which the life expectancy was only a few weeks." At least nine and probably more than twenty subjects died as a result of the experiment.

The studies at the University of Cincinnati began and continued after the medical literature clearly reflected that whole body irradiation was inappropriate. UC researchers preferentially selected patients with tumors that were not treatable by whole body irradiation (cancer of the colon, breast, and lung) and then told the patients that they would receive therapy for their disease.

TREATMENT OR ISOLATION

The experiment mimicked the effects of nuclear war on soldiers. The purpose of the experiments was as described in the researchers' reports to the Department of Defense: "These studies are designed to obtain new information about the metabolic effects of total body and partial body irradiation so as to have a better understanding of the acute and subacute effects of irradiation in the human...The long-term program envisions carrying out the various observations at dose levels of 100 to 150, and 300 rad. Eventually doses up to 600 rad are anticipated." These doses were potentially and were in fact lethal. Other physicians established this decades before the UC researchers conducted these experiments. A dose of 250 rads would kill up to 50% of those who received it. A 600 rad dose would kill almost everyone who received it.

From another DOD report we find that the researchers sought to psychologically isolate the patients: "There is no discussion with the patient of possible subjective reaction resulting from the treatment. Other physicians, nurses, technicians and ward personnel are instructed not to discuss post-irradiation symptoms or reactions with the patient. This 'isolation' is carried out carefully so as not to influence any objective reactions of the patient which might be attributable to radiation." Patients resided in the psychiatry unit instead of the tumor ward; "The environment is far more attractive, and there are no other patients receiving radiation therapy with whom the patient can exchange experiences." What manner of cancer treatment seeks to psychologically isolate patients and deny them treatment for nausea and vomiting?

WHY DID THIS HAPPEN?

It is my belief that we in the United States have a certain belief in the infallibility of our own history and our own behavior. We tend to believe that our actions could only have good intentions. I am afraid this is not so. We have at times done the wrong thing for the wrong reasons just as many other countries have done. The history of medical science, replete with the use of certain marginalized groups in our society for harmful experimentation, offers some examples of repugnant actions performed in this country. Perhaps these experiments will serve as a turning point and provide us with a fresh look at ourselves. A look that recognizes that the United States is the greatest country on earth but also recognizes that it is not an infallible country. That not everything we have done has been with good intentions or with good results, and therefore we, like other countries, must remain vigilant of our government, and our citizens and our companies. We must continue to maintain and buttress our system of checks and balances to assure us that these types of experiments will never go on again.

THE CINCINNATI EXPERIMENTS: THE COUNTERPOINT

Eugene L. Saenger

Eugene L. Saenger, M.D., is Professor Emeritus at the University of Cincinnati College of Medicine. Dr. Saenger directed the human radiation experiments at the University of Cincinnati/Cincinnati General Hospital from 1961-1972.

■ **POINTS TO CONSIDER**

1. Summarize Dr. Saenger's reasons for undertaking the research.

2. Discuss the procedures of informed consent according to Dr. Saenger. Do these comply with the Nuremberg Code in your opinion?

3. Compare and contrast Dr. Egilman and Dr. Saenger's versions of the appropriateness of treatment concerning nausea.

4. Why may Department of Defense funding be relevant to the question? According to Dr. Saenger, what role does DOD play?

5. How does Dr. Saenger defend his research from ethical attacks?

Excerpted from the testimony of Eugene L. Saenger, M.D., before the Subcommittee on Administrative Law and Government Relations of the House of Representatives Judiciary Committee, April 11, 1994.

In this project, the purpose and actual treatment and the possible outcomes were discussed with the patient and often included family members.

The primary goal of the study was to improve the treatment and general clinical management by increasing, if possible, survival of patients with advanced cancer and palliation of symptoms. (*Palliation* is treatment directed at relief but not cure.) In addition, observations and laboratory tests were carried out to seek effects of radiation on cancer patients and on the changes that could be ascribed to radiation.

The palliative effects of total body irradiation (TBI) were considered to be at least equal to and very likely to be superior to the chemotherapy available in the period from 1960 - 1970. Also the treatment methods were thought to be less stressful to the patients than chemotherapy then in use.

The background for this project originated in my observations over the prior 20 years that cancer patients treated with radiation might be benefitted by a more careful evaluation of the effects of this kind of treatment on the total patient.

It seemed to me at that time that the approach to the total management of the cancer patient receiving radiation therapy was not as well studied as was that of the same patient who would be treated surgically. In addition, the effect on the cancer patient of doses of radiation given through large fields in relation to systemic effects was not being adequately considered, even though much work was being done on the radiation effects on the tumor.

CATAPULTING THE RESEARCH

A major reason that we could begin total body radiation (TBI) and partial body radiation (PBI) resulted from several important developments. The cobalt 60 teletherapy unit was installed at General Hospital in 1958, the first in Ohio. Harold Perry, M.D., was the first full time radiation therapist at our hospital. He had come from Memorial-Sloan Kettering Cancer Center in New York Hospital and was familiar with TBI and PBI techniques and indicators. James G. Kereiakes, Ph.D., a physicist, joined the Department of Radiology in 1959. He calculated the doses, dose rate and distribution of radiation.

I believed that there could be implications from this treatment for well individuals exposed to radiation under other circumstances. In 1958, I submitted an unsolicited application to the Department of Defense (DOD), because there had been no studies on the metabolic effects of radiation and funds were available. This proposal was reviewed by J.A. Isherwood, M.D., for the Army Medical Research and Development Command. He made the following comments: "Any correlation of tumor response to total dose of irradiation by such means as proposed in this project would be of great value in the field of cancer. In addition if by some means such as those proposed, accurate knowledge of the total dose of radiation received could be determined, it would be of inestimable value in case of atomic disaster or nuclear warfare."

THE STUDY

Typical of medical investigations, this study progressed through phases. Patients were not recruited. Patients were referred for consideration for this form of therapy mostly from the Tumor Clinic (out-patient) and the Tumor Service (in-patient). I was not involved in patient selection or in determination of extent of therapy or dosage. These decisions were made solely by the attending physicians, internists and surgeons, and by radiation therapists. There were 24 patients entered into the study who were not given TBI or PBI. Some were rejected because it was thought that the patient would not benefit. Several patients and their families declined treatment.

Eligibility for therapy was spelled out in our 1962 document to the Department of Defense (DOD):

a.) There is a reasonable chance of therapeutic benefit to the patient. b.) The likelihood of damage to the patient is not greater than that encountered from comparable therapy of another type. c.) The facilities for support of the patient and complications of treatment offer all possible medical services for successful maintenance of the patient's well being. Race was not a factor in selection – only the type of cancer and its extent. A statistical analysis, done only after the program was terminated, confirmed that the patients in this study did not differ from the patient population of Cincinnati General Hospital. IQ was not a factor in patient selection.

INFORMED CONSENT

As in selection of patients, informed consent for therapy was obtained by the attending physicians. In the 1940s and 1950s informed consent was verbal except for the general brief informed consent required by the hospital from all patients to be hospitalized irrespective of the treatment to be administered. In this project, the purpose and actual treatment and the possible outcomes were discussed with the patient and often included family members.

In April 1965, the use of written informed consent, both for radiation and bone marrow harvesting and reinfusion, were developed by this project. These forms clearly indicated that risks of treatment were discussed. At that time, Department of Health Education and Welfare (DHEW) and DOD did not require written informed consent. As a result of a number of helpful suggestions from the University of Cincinnati Faculty Research Committee, several revisions to the form were made between 1967 and 1971. Furthermore, this written informed consent that we developed preceded any written requirements of the University of Cincinnati Medical Center by two years.

One criticism of our work stemmed from the instructions to the attending personnel not to inquire concerning nausea, vomiting and diarrhea in the first few days after treatment. We were particularly interested in the frequency of these manifestations. Since both nausea and vomiting could be induced by suggestive questions, we requested that no questions be asked as to how the patient felt. This restriction did not in any way restrict the administration of drugs such as Compazine to relieve symptoms. This care is amply documented in patients' charts. Of interest is that after treatment 39 patients (44%) had no nausea and vomiting, that 23 (27%) had symptoms for three hours or less and that 12 patients (14%) had symptoms for six hours or less. These responses are comparable to chemotherapy at the time, e.g., methotrexate, 5-fluorouacil and Chlorambucil.

FUNDING

As noted earlier, most costs of treatment were paid by Cincinnati General Hospital. An estimate of the expenditures for direct patient care for about 3,804 days at about $114 per day with some additional cost estimates gave a total calculated amount of $483,222. There were no professional costs or physician fees for patient care.

Some funding was obtained from the National Institutes of Health (NIH). Some patients were maintained on the General Clinical Research Center of Cincinnati General Hospital; this unit was supported by NIH. The protocols and records of each patient so hospitalized were submitted to the NIH and approved. In addition, several of the Post Graduate Fellows supported by the Radiation Training Grant of the National Institute of General Medical Sciences (NIH) participated in some phases of the program.

DOD funding was utilized solely for observation of patient symptoms and signs and for the extensive laboratory tests. DOD funds had no relation to choice of dose, choice of patient or patient care, in any way. No patient was compensated or reimbursed or paid for treatment. A Congressional General Accounting Office audit documented all of this in 1972. The total DOD contract for FY 1960 through FY 1971 was $671,482.79.

SUCCESS OF THE TBI STUDY

In the group of patients who received radiation, there were three categories in which there were enough patients to compare with other patients of the Cincinnati General Hospital treated differently or with comparable groups reported in the refereed medical literature. The cancers were those of the breast, lung and colon. The death rates were comparable to those treated by other means.

An important question is whether radiation was the factor leading to the early death of a patient. These patients had far advanced cancers which were growing exponentially. In the course of the disease, patients received chemotherapy and/or localized radiation therapy both before and immediately after TBI or PBI. For these reasons, it is not possible to identify a single form of treatment or the rapid growth of cancer as being the single contributing cause of death. It most likely would be the rate of growth of the cancer itself.

There were 20 cases in which patients survived longer than one year. Except for the one patient with Ewing's tumor who remains alive after 25 years, the longest survivor lived nine years. Two other relatively long survivors lived five years.

Palliation was successful with relief of pain in 31% of patients. Some decrease in tumor size occurred in 31% and an increase in well being was found in 30%. No change was observed in 31%. (In some patients there was more than one indication of improvement; thus the percentages exceed 100%).

REVIEW BY OTHERS

Our protocol was submitted to this newly formed Faculty Research Committee in March of 1966. Provisional approval was given in 1967 with recommendations for review of therapeutic efficacy, bone marrow infusion as a supportive measure and some revision in the study design. At no time was the project disapproved by the Faculty Research Committee as it received exhaustive and critical reviews.

The *ad hoc* Committee of the University of Cincinnati (the Suskind Report) undertook a complete review of the TBI project. Among the findings were that Phase III studies should be initiated with better criteria for the determination of palliative effects and that bone marrow transplantation be pursued. The study was judged to be adequate for support of the critically ill patients because of the development of skilled team management, especially with the help of the psychiatrist and psychologist coupled with home visits.

At the request of Senator Mike Gravel, the American College of Radiology formed an expert committee of Dr. Henry Kaplan,

Chairman of Radiology at Stanford University, Dr. Frank Hendrickson, Chairman of Radiation Therapy at Rush-Presbyterian Hospital, Chicago, and Dr. Samuel Taylor, III, a medical oncologist at Rush-Presbyterian Hospital, Chicago. This distinguished group made two visits to our hospital. Their major findings were as follows:

1. The project is validly conceived, stated, executed, controlled and followed up.

2. The process of patient selection based on clinical considerations conforms with good medical practice.

TBI SINCE 1971

It is apparently a common misunderstanding that the use of TBI/PBI as a therapeutic agent has been discontinued. In the period from 1970 to the present there have been major changes in the use of TBI and PBI. Doses have risen from the low levels of 100-300 rad TBI and up to 300 rad PBI used by us from 1960 to 1970. Doses now range from 600 to 1200 rad in single or divided doses of TBI. Fractionation has replaced single large doses (1200 rad) because of the complication of radiation pneumonitis. Among the solid tumors treated during these two decades have been cancer of breast, prostate, lung, colon and some sarcomas. At the University of Cincinnati Department of Radiation Oncology beginning in 1979, TBI and PBI were administered to adults and children for leukemias, lymphomas, cancers of breast and prostate and neuroblastoma. Non-malignant diseases treated included aplastic anemia and congenital anomalies.

EXAMINING COUNTERPOINTS

This activity may be used as an individualized study guide for students in libraries and resource centers or as a discussion catalyst in small group and classroom discussions.

The Point (see Reading 15)

The Counterpoint (see Reading 16)

Guidelines

Examine the counterpoints above and then consider the following questions:

1. Describe the nature and purpose of the Cincinnati Experiments.

2. Who are the authors? Discuss their professional backgrounds.

3. Summarize the arguments of both authors.

4. Do you agree more with the point or the counterpoint?

CHAPTER 5

RESEARCH AND ETHICS: THE PRINCIPLE OF INFORMED CONSENT

READING

17

INFORMED CONSENT: A BRIEF HISTORY

Irene Stith-Coleman

Irene Stith-Coleman is a Specialist in Life Sciences for the Congressional Research Service (CRS) with the Library of Congress.

■ POINTS TO CONSIDER

1. What events shaped the principle of informed consent? Previous to formal informed consent, what governed researchers?

2. Evaluate the Helsinki Code. What problems did it serve to address and create?

3. Discuss the drug thalidomide and how it affected the issue of informed consent in the United States.

4. Explain the history and function of the Institutional Review Board (IRB).

Excerpted from Irene Stith-Coleman, **Protection of Human Subjects in Research**, Washington, D.C.: Congressional Service, 1994.

The reports of human subject abuses in research during the 1960s and 1970s served as a catalyst for development of most, if not all, of the current requirements in this area.

INTERNATIONAL PRINCIPLES

Regulations and professional standards for the protection of human subjects in research and informed consent, for the most part, did not exist before the late 1940s. Reactions by the public, scientific community, and politicians in response to reports of human subject abuses in research during the 1960s and 1970s served as a catalyst for development of most, if not all, of the current requirements in this area.

THE HIPPOCRATIC OATH

Before the early 1940s, investigations with human subjects were conducted on a relatively small scale and primarily by physicians to treat the research subject (therapeutic). Standards to protect such human research subjects and to obtain informed consent were nebulous. Before the early 1940s, the medical community's responsibility to human research subjects derived largely from the Hippocratic Oath, the first set of Western writings about medical professional conduct.

This set of professional standards does not address essential issues of the physician's ethical research responsibility, such as the role of informed consent in the patient-physician relationship, or the roles of communication and disclosure. Instead, the physician is presumed to have special beneficence skills and ethical commitments to their use when treating patients. The Oath discusses a number of problems associated with truth-telling by the physician, advising him of the wisdom of "concealing most things from the patient, while you are attending to him...turning his attention away from what is being done to him...revealing nothing of the patient's future or present condition."

THE NUREMBERG CODE

The Nuremberg Code is a set of 10 ethical research principles that originated from the Nuremberg tribunal held in 1945 and 1946. The code was produced as part of the judgment against

Nazi physicians who engaged in atrocious medical experiments on non-consenting concentration camp prisoners during World War II. Many of the convicted physicians had been university-trained, were university-appointed researchers, and had first-rate medical credentials and sought distinguished careers.

The first Nuremberg Code principle states, without qualification, that "the voluntary consent of the human subject is absolutely essential. This means that the person involved should have the legal capacity to give consent." Principle 1, therefore, requires that consent have at least four characteristics: it must be voluntary, competent, informed, and comprehending. The remainder of Principle 1 assigns general boundaries within which a researcher may conduct investigations and defines the conditions under which a subject has the ability to volunteer.

PROTECTIONS FOR THE VULNERABLE

It is worthy of note, as well, that vulnerable populations such as the mentally disabled and prisoners were at that time in some cases being used as research subjects by American researchers. This practice was inconsistent with the Code's principle that subjects should have legal capacity to give consent, and be so situated as to be able to exercise free power of choice. However, few of these issues received sustained evaluation in the United States at that time. The ethical principles generated at Nuremberg did not appear to have a significant impact on the U.S. research establishment until several years after the development of the Nuremberg Code.

THE HELSINKI CODE

Over time, the medical research community perceived the gruesome experiments at Nuremberg as a potential threat to the integrity and reputation of biomedical research. In 1964, partially in reaction to this perception, the World Medical Association (WMA) adopted the Helsinki Code. This code, the first one prescribed internally by a medical professional body, also includes informed consent as an essential requirement of clinical research involving humans. However, the Helsinki Code makes an important distinction between therapeutic and non-therapeutic research.

Therapeutic research, defined as research "combined with professional care," is permitted if in the physician's judgment, "it offers hope of saving life, reestablishing health, or alleviating suffering." Non-therapeutic research is defined as purely scientific research with no therapeutic benefit to the subject. In the latter case, the purpose of the research and risk associated with it must be explained to the subject. In addition, voluntary consent must be obtained from the subject; unless the subject is incompetent, in which case guardian consent should be obtained.

The Helsinki Code does not require informed consent in therapeutic research if consent is not "consistent with patient psychology." The justification for this broad exception is similar to the beneficence-based assumption that supports the physician's therapeutic privilege in the Hippocratic Oath. If a physician considers it essential not to obtain consent, then he must state the specific reasons in the experimental protocol, which are transmitted to an independent committee. Some commentators refer to this provision as a so-called "therapeutic loophole," and identify it as a serious flaw. In particular, this is of concern in cases where an inattentive review committee might examine research protocols.

FDA AND THALIDOMIDE

The first Federal statute related to informed consent focused on the Food and Drug Administration (FDA). On October 10, 1962, Congress passed the "Drug Amendments of 1962" (P.L. 87-781), section 505(i) of the Food, Drug, and Cosmetic Act. The law contains a "consent requirement," the genesis of which was due largely to the thalidomide disaster.

In 1962, it became evident, first in Europe, that thalidomide was harmful to the fetus. Some babies were born with a rare defect known as *phocomelia* (infants' limbs are missing or a hand or foot is attached directly to the body). However, by then, 20,000 Americans, 3,750 of childbearing age and 624 reportedly pregnant, had already taken the drug. The exact number of recipients was not known and identification was incomplete, in part because inadequate records were kept by the drug maker and the prescribing physicians.

FDA published regulations to implement P.L. 87-781 on February 7, 1963. The "consent" provision required researchers proposing to test investigational new drugs to obtain human subjects' consent, or that of their representatives, "except where they deem it not feasible, or in their professional judgment, contrary to the best interests of such human beings." Critics claimed that the

HUMAN RADIATION EXPERIMENTS:
The Department of Energy Roadmap to the Story and the Records – 1995

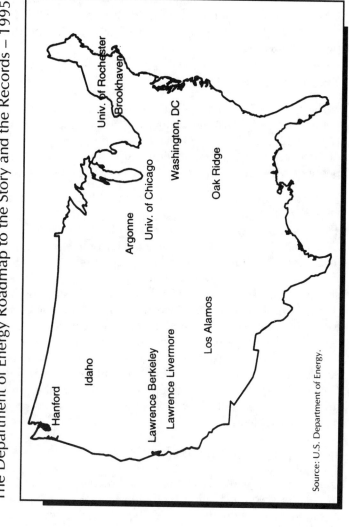

Source: U.S. Department of Energy.

consent provisions of the regulations were poorly developed and led to ambiguities.

On February 8, 1966, the U.S. Surgeon General published a policy directive requiring institutional review to assure ethical acceptability of research with human subjects. This policy, "Clinical Investigations Using Human Subjects," required all institutions receiving Federal grant funding from the Public Health Service (PHS) to provide prior review by a committee for proposed investigations with human subjects.

THE TUSKEGEE STUDY

The 1972 PHS Committee was created largely in response to the publicizing of the Tuskegee Study, which was funded by the PHS. From 1932 until 1972, PHS investigators had performed a variety of tests and medical examinations on the men – 399 with final phase of syphilis, and 201 men who were free of the disease.

Shortly after the media reported the Tuskegee Study, the Department of Health, Education and Welfare (DHEW)appointed an *ad hoc* advisory panel to review both the study and the Department's policies and procedures for protecting human subjects generally. The panel found in its report released in 1973 that the study was ethically unjustified, and that penicillin therapy should have been made available to all study subjects no later than 1953, 19 years before the study was halted. The panel also found that neither DHEW, nor any other government agency had policy in place to adequately review experimental procedures, or to adequately obtain informed consent from research subjects. Among other things, the *ad hoc* panel recommended that Congress create a permanent body with authority, at a minimum, to regulate all federally supported and conducted research involving human subjects.

INSTITUTIONAL REVIEW BOARDS

On May 30, 1974, DHEW published regulations governing the protection of human subjects, thereby replacing the policy the agency first developed in 1966. The old policy review requirements applied only to research activities judged by the principal investigator to present risk to human subjects, while the 1974 regulations applied to all research with human subjects. The Institutional Review Board (IRB), and not investigators, would now determine the extent of any risk involved.

Each institution that conducts research involving human subjects must first submit written "assurance" satisfactory to the department or agency head that it will comply with the requirements. The assurance should include a statement of principles (e.g., Nuremburg Code, Helsinki Code) the institution will follow to accomplish its responsibilities for protecting human subjects in research conducted or supported by the institution. The institution also must certify that the research has been reviewed and approved, and will be subject to continuing review by an IRB provided for in the assurance.

The IRB must be composed of a minimum of five members (in the local area) who have varying backgrounds. The members must be sufficiently qualified through experience and expertise to promote complete and adequate review of research activities commonly conducted by the institution. IRB members must be identified to the Department of Health and Human Services (DHHS) by name, earned degree, representative capacity, and evidence of experience (i.e., board certification, license).

In carrying out specified responsibilities, the IRB must review all research activities involving human research subjects. IRB members have authority to approve, require modifications (to secure approval), or disapprove all such research activities. They must assure that informed consent information given to research subjects is in accordance with requirements. In addition, they can require that information, in addition to that specified in the regulations, be given to subjects if, in their judgment, it would meaningfully add to the protection and welfare of subjects.

18

THE UCLA SCHIZOPHRENIA STUDY WAS UNETHICAL

Robert, Gloria and Gregory Aller

Robert, Gloria and Greg Aller composed the following report in response to the Office for Protection from Research Risks (OPRR) final report on the UCLA Schizophrenia Study. Robert and Gloria Aller filed the original complaint against UCLA to OPRR in April 1991 on behalf of their son, Greg. They oppose the conclusion of OPRR concerning the ethical justifiability of the study.

■ POINTS TO CONSIDER

1. Discuss what happened to Greg Aller.

2. Summarize the events that led the Allers to question UCLA and the study.

3. Why do the Allers believe the study is inherently flawed?

4. Do you agree with this?

Excerpted from Robert, Gloria and Gregory Aller, "Rebuttal from Robert, Gloria and Gregory Aller to OPRR Evaluation of Human Protection in Schizophrenia Research conducted by the University of California, Los Angeles, " March 25, 1994.

How can research that intentionally harms people without their consent be considered "scientifically and ethically justifiable?"

In 1966, Henry K. Beecher's landmark paper, "Ethics in Clinical Research," was published in the *New England Journal of Medicine,* 274 (1966):1354-60. Example #5 in Beecher's paper described one of a number of experiments that Beecher considered to be unethical. Example #5 was research taking place at the University of California, Los Angeles Center for Health Sciences (UCLA Medical Center).

Beecher made additional comments that we find relevant to the ongoing UCLA experimentation on subjects/patients with schizophrenia. "Ordinary patients will not knowingly risk their health or their life for the sake of science...I have worked on the ward of a large hospital for 35 years, and I know perfectly well that ward patients will not volunteer for any such use of themselves for experimental purposes when the hazard may be permanent injury or death." (Beecher to Joseph Sadusk, Medical Director, Food and Drug Administration (FDA).) Beecher's words have particular meaning today. In plain language, the researchers were planning to carefully track the long-term deterioration or disintegration of their patients.

BACKGROUND

By January 1990, after the withdrawal of anti-psychotic medication by UCLA schizophrenia researchers, our son, Gregory began to suffer what became an extremely severe and dangerous psychotic relapse.

Despite our written and oral pleas, medication was not reinstated by the researchers until May of 1990. After discussing the research with an expert in methodology, we became concerned that there might be some methodological or human error problems in the conduct of the research program. We began asking for protocols and grant applications, but the researchers were not responsive to our requests.

By December 1990, though Greg was taking his medication, he had still not returned to his former level of functioning. We saw that the effects of relapse were still profound, and we decided to bring the problems to the appropriate UCLA administrators.

DEFICIENT METHODOLOGY

On February 20, 1991, we met with the Vice Chancellor of Research Programs, Albert Barber, Ph.D., the Chairperson of the Human Subject Protection Committee (HSPC), Frederick Montz, M.D., and the administrator of the HSPC, Gitta Walton. We explained that we believed there were methodological problems or human error in measuring relapse in the schizophrenic research project conducted by Keith Nuechterlein, Ph.D., and Michael Gitlin, M.D. Based on our experience with our son, we explained that we believed that a murder or suicide would occur if UCLA didn't intervene in the conduct of the research. With a letter from Gregory, we requested a copy of all of Gregory's patient records. We told Drs. Barber and Montz and Gitta Walton that we would have the records examined by experts at other institutions to determine precisely what had happened.

As graduates of UCLA, Gloria and I explained that we did not have any intention of bringing a lawsuit against UCLA; we merely wanted to correct what we thought might be some problems with the research. Finally, after additional requests, on March 11, 1991, a few of Gregory's patient records were provided to us. A "Medication Record" looked as if it had "white-outs," obliterations and alterations on the record. So, on March 12, 1991, we went with the Ombudsperson for the Neuropsychiatric Institute and the Acting Director for the Aftercare Clinic, and we viewed the original "Medication Record." We verified that the alterations, obliterations and white-outs existed on the original record. By calling other hospital record departments in Los Angeles, we learned that the use of white-outs, obliterations and alterations was a wholly unacceptable standard for any hospital, medical center, or research institution.

We contacted Vice Chancellor Barber regarding these new problems, but he referred us to the Campus Counsel, Patricia Jasper. Though the consent we had signed stated that any complaints should be addressed to Dr. Barber, the form did not state that Dr. Barber had any obligation to respond. In fact, Dr. Barber has never spoken to us since that first meeting.

UCLA maintained a position of refusing to provide the balance of our son's patient records and out of sheer frustration, with no one else to turn to, we discovered that there was an office at the National Institutes of Health (NIH) expressly for the protection of

> # T.D. VERSUS NEW YORK STATE OFFICE OF MENTAL HEALTH
>
> Defendants-Appellants-Respondents (Defendants) were performing high risk, wholly non-therapeutic experiments on incapacitated patients in psychiatric facilities without the patients' consent and sometimes without the patients' knowledge. Defendants' use of patients as human guinea pigs is not only unethical, but it violates the most basic precepts of the state and federal Constitution, the common law and New York's Public Health Law. If human dignity and control of one's life and body are to have meaning, this Court must prevent Defendants from trampling the rights of our most vulnerable citizens.
>
> T.D. et al. versus New York State Office of Mental Health, Supreme Court, State of New York Appellate Division; First Department, Brief for Plaintiffs-Respondents-Appellants, p. 1.

human subjects. In mid-March, 1991, we contacted the Office for Protection from Research Risks (OPRR), who naturally told us to put our allegation in writing. While we were drafting our allegation of no legally valid informed consent, another tragedy occurred in the program.

FELLOW SUBJECT COMMITS SUICIDE

On March 28,1991, Tony Lamadrid, a fellow patient with Gregory, jumped off the engineering building, committing suicide. We soon learned that Tony had been withdrawn from medication after being asked to leave the program. We met with Tony's brothers.

Gregory, Gloria and I had many questions. Why would a psychiatrist, Dr. Michael Gitlin, initial records that had white-outs, obliterations and alterations? What could lead up to the failure of the researchers to try to prevent Tony Lamadrid's suicide? What other kinds of adverse outcomes might have occurred in this research program?

Under the Freedom of Information Act, we obtained the grant applications, summary reports, protocols and other related documents. We also read all of the papers published by the researchers. It became clear to us why the researchers had not heeded our pleas for the reinstatement of medication. The primary aim of the study was to measure the effects of psychotic relapse on patients. Now, three years later, OPRR has issued its report.

SUMMARY RESPONSE TO THE OPRR REPORT

We appreciate that the Office for Protection from Research Risks (OPRR) has rebuked the UCLA researchers for their failure to obtain legally valid informed consent. However, we believe that the OPRR report condones the researchers' deliberate harming of vulnerable patients (without informed consent). By failing to conduct an objective fact-finding investigation, OPRR colludes with NIH in exonerating the serious harm to subjects.

In particular, we object to the OPRR finding that the UCLA research was "scientifically and ethically justifiable." OPRR never acknowledged that relapse was an integral part of the research design. How can research that intentionally harms people without their consent be considered "scientifically and ethically justifiable?"

PROTECTING THE DOCTORS, NOT THE SUBJECTS/PATIENTS

Before we offer our critique of the investigation and conclusions, we have a few comments. After viewing the grant applications, protocols and published papers, we drew our conclusions as lay readers. Then, we provided the documents to psychiatrists, psychologists and bioethicists who confirmed our conclusions. But, it took three long years to bring these facts to light. Why?

One expert hypothesized that it was difficult for people to accept the fact that some research, by its very design, will harm patients. The common perception has always been that doctors try to do their best for patients. It is, indeed difficult to accept the harsh reality that the Hippocratic oath of "Do No Harm" has been cast aside by some researchers – in the "name of science."

Two years ago a science reporter asked us why OPRR didn't close the project upon learning that no informed consent was obtained. OPRR could have protected subjects from harm while conducting the lengthy investigation. But, unfortunately, for subjects, that is not the way the system currently works. What this rebuttal attempts to express is our belief that there is no governmental entity that truly protects human subjects. The pressures from the research establishment protect the researchers, not the subjects. For example, one renowned psychiatrist in schizophrenia had helped us for two years until pressures were applied. He had to withdraw his support.

THE INVISIBLE RESEARCH SUBJECTS

Our son, Gregory, had been withdrawn from medication in this research, and he had suffered an extremely severe relapse. His cognitive functioning has not returned to the level of functioning he had achieved before the relapse. (3.8 GPA at college and working 15 hours a week.) His loss of functioning has been a constant reminder of the negative impact of the UCLA research. We wish to point out that Greg has never had a relapse since he left the UCLA program, and he has been taking anti-psychotic medication every day.

And yet, Greg's adverse experience pales by comparison to the experiences of other patients we are familiar with. Tragically, Tony Lamadrid committed suicide after he was asked to leave the program and his medication was taken away. Even after Tony told his case worker that he planned to commit suicide, the UCLA staff failed to contact his family. They did tell Tony to check himself into a hospital, hardly an appropriate response to a severely depressed, suicidal patient with schizophrenia, whose condition had been exacerbated by removal of anti-psychotic medication. The staff knew just how depressed Tony was at the loss of his connection to the program, and five years of friendships with other patients. The research staff could have easily hospitalized Tony on an involuntary basis. A brochure handed to patients told them they would receive the optimal dose of medication. Not true. Patients had been deceived from day one.

These are faces and people and families who were harmed while the researchers were collecting data that advanced their careers and brought significant research funds to the University. In our view, the researchers lost sight of the fact that they were experimenting on human beings, with needs and aspirations and lives. The researchers used the lives of the subjects for their own professional career needs. The researchers failed to consider the havoc that they could wreak on the families.

READING

19

THE UCLA SCHIZOPHRENIA STUDY WAS ETHICALLY JUSTIFIED

Office for Protection from Research Risks

The Office for Protection from Research Risks (OPRR) is the arm of the National Institutes of Health (NIH) which investigates claims of violation against basic rights for human research subjects. OPRR began investigating allegations of violation in a UCLA schizophrenia study brought by Robert and Gloria Aller, parents of a subject in the study, in April 1991.

■ **POINTS TO CONSIDER**

1. Describe the design of the UCLA experiment.

2. Summarize the allegations against the UCLA study. How does the University initially respond?

3. Discuss the issues which OPRR addresses in its investigation of the study.

4. With respect to informed consent requirements, does the University comply, according to the findings?

5. Identify a possible conflict of interest in the study. What does OPRR say about this?

Excerpted from "Evaluation of Human Subject Protections in Schizophrenia Research Conducted by the University of California Los Angeles." Office for Protection from Research Risks, May 11, 1994.

Examination of available information revealed no basis for rejecting the UCLA determination that the design of the Schizophrenic Disorders research is scientifically and ethically justifiable.

On April 4, 1991, the Office for Protection from Research Risks (OPRR) received allegations that schizophrenia research conducted by the University of California Los Angeles (UCLA) and supported by the National Institute of Mental Health (NIMH, grant MH37705, "Developmental Processes in Schizophrenic Disorders") had failed to comply with Health and Human Services (HHS) regulations for the protection of human research subjects.

Funding for the UCLA Schizophrenic Disorders research was originally awarded by the NIMH in September 1983 and continues to the present. The research includes two treatment protocols. The first protocol (Protocol I: "Developmental Processes in Outcome") involves treatment of recent-onset schizophrenic subjects with a fixed dosage of an injectable anti-psychotic medication every two weeks for a period of one year. The second protocol (Protocol II) involves discontinuation of this medication. Subjects must have completed Protocol I to be eligible for Protocol II.

INITIAL ALLEGATIONS

Over a period of several months beginning in April 1991, letters and telephone calls from two separate complainants raised several potentially serious issues related to the treatment of human subjects in UCLA's Schizophrenic Disorders research.

One issue involved the alleged failure on the part of UCLA to obtain legally effective informed consent from research subjects, as required under HHS regulations. OPRR was particularly concerned about allegations that informed consent documents for the research inappropriately omitted description of reasonably foreseeable risks to subjects, particularly risks associated with the withdrawal of neuroleptic medication. OPRR was also concerned about suggestions that investigators had purposely underestimated the risks to subjects in protocols submitted to the UCLA Institutional Review Board (IRB).

A second issue involved UCLA's alleged failure to minimize the potential risks of the research to subjects, resulting in the apparent suicide of one subject and the psychotic relapse of another. Under HHS regulations, IRBs are required to determine that risks to subjects are minimized by using procedures that are consistent with sound research design and do not unnecessarily expose subjects to risk. IRBs must also determine that risks are reasonable in relation to anticipated benefits, and that the research plan makes adequate provision for monitoring data to ensure the safety of subjects.

OPRR was concerned about allegations that the research design exposed subjects to unnecessary risks and that data monitoring was inadequate to ensure safety, especially during the medication withdrawal phase of the research. It was alleged that the design of the research virtually guaranteed psychotic relapse, and that reasonable monitoring and intervention to prevent relapse were purposely withheld from subjects. A related concern was the allegation that the research failed to include safeguards sufficient to protect the rights and welfare of a potentially vulnerable category of subjects (i.e., subjects suffering from severe psychiatric disorders), as required under HHS regulations.

Additional issues involved record keeping for the research. It was alleged that UCLA had failed to maintain proper medical and research records and that records contained inappropriate alterations. It was also alleged that UCLA had failed to provide subjects with medical information and medical records as required under State law.

UCLA RESPONSE

UCLA officials reviewed the Schizophrenic Disorders research and provided written responses to these issues in May and October 1991. UCLA indicated to OPRR that the research had received continuous review and approval by the full IRB since 1982 and pointed out that its IRB included both a psychiatrist and a psychologist. UCLA stated that the risks of clinical relapse and psychotic exacerbation were clearly presented to the IRB by the investigators. UCLA also stated that the investigators had reported all observed outcomes to the IRB annually, including statistics regarding relapse, and that no other unanticipated problems had occurred during research participation.

UCLA disputed the allegation that a subject had committed suicide as the result of participation in the research. UCLA indicated that the individual in question had completed research participa-

tion and was being seen only "as a patient in a treatment program" at the time of death. UCLA maintained that risks to subjects were appropriate, as were measures for monitoring data to ensure subject safety. UCLA also noted that early intervention in psychotic exacerbation cases (i.e., prior to clinical relapse) was "a primary method for reducing risks," and that NIMH peer reviews had repeatedly found human subject protections to be adequate.

UCLA's July 1992 response to OPRR reiterated that the Schizophrenic Disorders research had several times undergone extensive peer review as part of the initial and continuing NIMH application/award process. UCLA made clear that the Aftercare Program is an "entry point" for research and that persons who do not consent to research participation or who do not adapt to protocol conditions are referred to alternate treatment programs. UCLA indicated that this arrangement is communicated to all potential enrollees, and that a modification of the Aftercare Program brochure to that effect was in progress.

UCLA noted that since 1989, informed consent documents for the Developmental Processes protocol had included the following statement: I understand that I will be given a standard dosage of a widely used anti-psychotic medication, prolixin decanoate, 12.5 mg. every two weeks, during my first outpatient year of participation in this project. This dosage will not be changed unless I develop symptoms that indicate that a medication change is necessary.

UCLA also stated that the standard medication dosage can be

lowered if intolerable side effects occur and that subjects who cannot be clinically stabilized within the initial months of outpatient treatment are referred to other treatment programs. UCLA maintained that subjects are fully informed about the issues raised by OPRR through the Aftercare Program's "verbal informed consent process." Nevertheless, UCLA agreed to expand the written informed consent documents for the Development Processes protocol to address OPRR's various concerns.

FINDINGS

As indicated previously, OPRR's evaluation of human subject protections in the UCLA Schizophrenic Disorders research addressed five broad areas of concern: (a) informed consent and IRB review; (b) research risks, data monitoring, and intervention to prevent relapse (including current scientific knowledge and standards for clinical treatment); (c) record keeping; (d) subject access to medical and research records; and (e) the participation of Subjects "A" and "B" in the research. Findings in each of these areas are described below.

HHS regulations clearly require "a written consent document that embodies the elements of informed consent" stipulated in the regulations, unless (a) the IRB has waived this requirement in accordance with the criteria specified in the regulations, or (b) the institution has met the conditions prescribed in the regulations for utilizing "short form" documentation of elements presented orally. Neither of these exceptions to the requirement for a written consent document are applicable to the Schizophrenic Disorders research.

Consequently, OPRR finds that, prior to September 1992, the IRB-approved consent documents for UCLA's Schizophrenic Disorders research failed to comply with the requirements of HHS regulations in that they omitted certain basic elements required for legally effective informed consent as defined under the regulations. Specifically, OPRR finds that these informed consent documents failed to contain (a) adequate description of the procedures to be followed in the research; (b) adequate description of reasonably foreseeable risks of the research; and (c) adequate disclosure of appropriate alternative procedures or courses of treatment that might be advantageous to the subject, as required under HHS regulations.

OPRR further finds (a) that the UCLA School of Medicine IRB erred in not requiring inclusion of the above required elements in the written informed consent documents for the Schizophrenic Disorders research, and (b) that provision of information to subjects through the extended oral informed consent process described by UCLA did not satisfy the requirements of HHS regulations.

INTERVENTION TO PREVENT RELAPSE

OPRR's examination of available information and records revealed no demonstrable basis for rejecting the UCLA IRB's determination that the methodological design of the Schizophrenic Disorders research is scientifically and ethically justifiable. Research and data monitoring procedures appear to incorporate current scientific knowledge and standards for clinical treatment. Summary data concerning the actual medication dosage levels received by subject experiencing psychotic exacerbation and relapse during their participation in the Schizophrenic Disorders research were examined by OPRR and by the two expert consultants who participated in OPRR's March 1993 meeting with the UCLA investigators. These summary data appear to be consistent with procedures that incorporate current scientific knowledge and standards for clinical treatment.

RECORD KEEPING

OPRR's examination of altered and nonchronological entries in records made available during the March 1993 meeting did not reveal evidence of risk or harm to research subjects. However, OPRR finds certain record keeping practices for the Schizophrenic Disorders research to be unsatisfactory, including (a) the procedures for altering entries when there is some ambiguity in determining appropriate rating, and (b) the procedures for correcting errors made in transcribing data.

PARTICIPATION OF SUBJECTS "A" AND "B" IN THE SCHIZOPHRENIC DISORDERS RESEARCH

OPRR's examination of information and records made available by UCLA revealed no evidence that the clinical treatment of Subjects "A" and "B" during their involvement in the Schizophrenic Disorders research failed to adhere to currently accepted clinical standards.

It must be noted, however, that both subjects participated in the research, at least in part, on the basis of informed consent documents that OPRR had found deficient. Although Subject "A" was no longer participating in either of the two Schizophrenic Disorders research treatment protocols at the time of death, this subject remained an Aftercare Program participant whose clinical monitoring data were available for research purposes. Thus, Subject "A" continued to be an Aftercare Program research participant.

Based on its contacts with the complainants in this case, who are family members of the subjects referenced above, OPRR has identified a need for written informational material specifically describing the role of family members in Aftercare Program research and clinical treatment.

WAIVING INFORMED CONSENT: THE POINT

Food and Drug Administration

The Food and Drug Administration (FDA) released new regulations November 1, 1996, concerning informed consent. The regulations will allow patients with life-threatening conditions unable to give consent to be enrolled in medical research studies. The following article from the Federal Register *discusses the history and proposal of the new regulation.*

■ POINTS TO CONSIDER

1. Define "deferred consent." Why is this concept troublesome to Health and Human Services (HHS)?

2. In what situations are there conflicts between informed consent and research? How does the FDA propose to solve this?

3. Summarize the three basic principles that apply to human research, according to the Belmont Report.

4. Evaluate the contention that waivers of informed consent in emergency research can help create "equitable distribution" in research.

5. What does "equitable distribution" mean?

Food and Drug Administration, Health and Human Services, "Protection of Human Subjects; Informed Consent; Proposed Rule," **Federal Register**, vol. 60, no. 183, September 21, 1995: 49086-103.

Waiving the requirement for informed consent from potential subjects and their surrogates helps to provide for an equitable distribution of both burdens and benefits of emergency research.

By permitting certain adequate and well-controlled clinical trials to occur that involve human subjects who are confronted by a life-threatening condition and who also are unable to give informed consent because of that condition, the agency expects the clinical trials in these situations will allow people access to potentially life-saving therapies and will result in advancement in knowledge and improvement of therapies used in emergency medical situations. Most therapeutic intervention in acute care and emergency research must be initiated immediately to be life-saving. For victims of heart attacks or head injuries, for example, this intervention often must be instituted in the field, prior to hospital admission, when the individual is usually found to be unresponsive and unable to communicate, and where there usually is no authorized representative of the subject available to give surrogate consent.

In 1993, the agency became aware that certain Institutional Review Boards (IRBs) were approving research involving interventions in acutely life-threatening situations by invoking a "deferred consent" procedure. This term was used to describe a procedure whereby subjects or representatives of subjects are informed, after the fact, that the subject participated, unknowingly, in a clinical investigation of an experimental product, and was administered a test article in the course of the investigation. Subjects or their representatives were then asked to ratify that participation retroactively, and to agree to continuing participation. As described, "deferred consent" is nothing other than *post hoc* ratification. *Post hoc* ratification is not genuine consent because the subject or representative has no opportunity to prevent the administration of the test article, and cannot, therefore meaningfully be said to have consented to its use. Thus, although the research community is now aware that "deferred consent" does not constitute valid informed consent, it has been given no alternative procedure under which it may conduct emergency research under the Food and Drug Administration (FDA) and Health and Human Services (HHS) regulations.

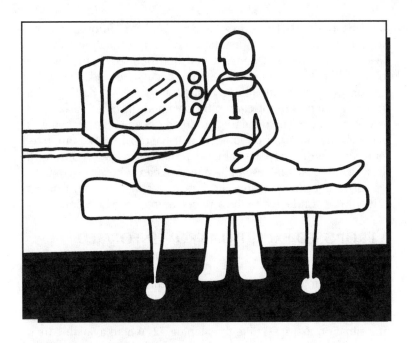

SUPPORT FOR CHANGE

In correspondence, at meetings, and in published articles, the IRB and research communities have expressed their frustration at the difficulties they face in interpreting existing regulations to fit the needs of emergency research. They have identified the need for the FDA and the National Insitutes of Health (NIH) to reach a decision concerning the conduct of these studies. Patient advocacy groups and researchers have stressed that the research at stake is of great importance to patients and the health of the nation and care must be taken to ensure that the agencies' regulations do not inappropriately disrupt access to, or prevent the development of, potentially life-saving treatments for serious illnesses and injuries.

SMALL FRACTION

The research addressed by this proposed regulation is believed to constitute a small fraction of all clinical research. This is because, in some instances, an individual may be unconscious or incompetent to give informed consent, but immediate involvement in research is not needed to promote healing or to prevent death. In those instances, it may be possible to delay participation in research until consent from a legally authorized representative can be obtained. There are also medical conditions that predictably occur in given identifiable patient populations. In such cases, prior informed consent can be obtained from potential future subjects before the intervention occurs, because the patient will understand the likelihood of the future need to participate in research when consent cannot be obtained. In other cases, such as events that occur regularly in already hospitalized, acutely ill patients, the majority of subjects will have a legally authorized representative readily available to provide surrogate consent. In these instances, the research may proceed without invoking a waiver of informed consent. In those cases that remain, research can only be conducted in the absence of informed consent.

A PROPOSED EXCEPTION FROM INFORMED CONSENT

The exception from the informed consent requirement permitted by the proposed rule would be conditioned upon various findings by an Institutional Review Board (IRB). First, the subject must be in a situation that is: (1) life-threatening, (2) where available treatments are unproven or unsatisfactory, and (3) the collection of valid scientific evidence is necessary to determine the most beneficial intervention. In addition, the opportunity to be in the study must be in the interest of the subject, because the life-threatening situation necessitates intervention, and the risk of the study is reasonable in light of the medical condition. With regard to the study itself, it must be research that could not practicably be carried out without the informed consent waiver.

ETHICAL BASIS FOR THESE REGULATIONS

In developing this proposed regulation, FDA has carefully considered the basic ethical principles that underlie research to ensure that it is consistent with those principles. The agency is convinced that the research described in this section is ethically permissible.

The current informed consent regulations are based, in large part, on the ethical principles discussed in the Belmont Report. As discussed in that report, the three basic ethical principles that are relevant to research involving human subjects are the principles of respect for persons, beneficence, and justice.

The principle of respect for persons incorporates two general rules of ethical behavior: (1) Competent individuals must be treat-

NEW RULES

For the first time in a half-century, new federal regulations allow investigators to enroll some patients in some medical research studies without their consent...FDA regulations apply only in carefully circumscribed situations. The patients must have a life-threatening condition, such as a severe head injury, and must be unable to say whether they want to be part of a study. They would be selected only if it was not feasible to obtain consent from a relative...

The new rules arose out of the frustration of some ethicists and medical researchers. The problem was that the previous rules were making it virtually impossible to study treatments that must be provided to patients who are gravely ill or injured, with heart attacks, strokes or head injuries, for example, for whom time is of the essence, and whose relatives cannot be found in time to give permission for experimental treatments. At the same time, scientists were testing seemingly nontoxic drugs in animals that promised to save the lives of many of these patients.

"Research Without Patient Consent Now Allowed," 1996 **News Services**.

ed as autonomous agents, that is to say, persons who are legally and morally competent to understand the risks and benefits of a proposed research activity must provide prior, uncoerced informed consent before they may be enrolled as research subjects; and (2) persons whose autonomy is absent or diminished may participate in research only if additional protections are provided for them. The proposed rule recognizes that subjects who are candidates for emergency research will not meet the condition of being fully competent. In many cases, they will be totally incompetent. Such potential subjects, if they are to be enrolled in research, must be provided with special additional protections. The special protections proposed in this rule for subjects of emergency research include prior Food and Drug Administration (FDA) and community consultation on the research, public disclosure, and careful mandatory oversight of the welfare of subjects by a data and safety monitoring board.

The principle of beneficence requires that the risks associated with a research activity are reasonable in the light of expected benefits. It also requires that the chance for benefits from participation be maximized, and the risk of possible harm be minimized, consistent with sound research design.

INCREASING MINORITY PARTICIPATION

The principle of justice requires that the burdens and benefits of participation in research be equitably distributed across the entire population in the place or region where the research is conducted. That means, in general, that racial, ethnic, gender, and economic status should not be used as exclusion criteria for participation in research. It further means that persons who are eligible for participation in the research because of their disease or condition should be provided reasonable opportunity to participate in research until the research cohort is fully recruited. Experience has repeatedly shown that requiring surrogate consent from legally authorized representatives tends to inhibit equitable inclusion in the study because surrogate consent is more easily obtained from family members of Caucasians than from family members of minorities, and it is more easily obtained from family members of middle and upper income persons than from persons of lower income. Waiving the requirement for informed consent from potential subjects and their surrogates helps to provide for an equitable distribution of both burdens and benefits of emergency research in a manner that meets the requirements of justice.

The principle of justice is also pertinent to this proposed rule. Systematically excluding persons who are unable to give informed consent and who have no surrogate to consent for them from research may be discriminatory, as noted above. An inability to consent, or lack of an authorized representative, should not in itself be a reason for excluding persons from participating in potentially beneficial and scientifically well-designed, controlled, studies.

The Proposed Rule will be applicable only to limited research activities that involve individuals who are in a life-threatening situation and for whom available treatments are unproven or unsatisfactory. FDA believes that evidence submitted at the Public Forum on the chilling effect of current regulations on the care and medical management of such persons in life-threatening situations, including impairing their access to potentially life-saving therapy, justifies the prompt issuance of regulations governing research on such subjects.

READING

21

WAIVING INFORMED CONSENT: THE COUNTERPOINT

Jay Katz

Jay Katz, M.D., Yale Law School, has been an advocate on the issue of basic rights of research subjects for 30 years. He was a member of the ad hoc Advisory Committee for the Tuskegee Syphilis Study.

■ POINTS TO CONSIDER

1   Discuss the reasons Katz opposes waivers of informed consent from local Institutional Review Boards (IRBs) for incompetent patients.

2. Evaluate the Katz position on "deferred consent."

3. What alternative does the author propose for the changed rules on informed consent?

Excerpted from the testimony of Jay Katz before the Subcommittee on Regulation, Business Opportunities and Technology of the House of Representatives Committee on Small Business, May 23, 1994.

Federal regulations on informed consent are in need of a thoroughgoing reevaluation from many perspectives. Most generally, the informed consent requirement should emphasize that taking informed consent seriously in research negotiations obligates physician-investigators to spend considerable time with patient-subjects.

Informed consent is largely meaningless when research with mentally incompetent patient-subjects in emergency rooms is at issue. In these situations we must confront a number of questions: (1) how should the tensions between the protection of human subjects , on the one hand, and the advancement of knowledge, on the other, be resolved; (2) in these situations can patient-subjects ever be recruited for the sake of science; and (3) if so, who should be invested with the authority to make such awesome decisions?

I do not believe that local Institutional Review Boards (IRBs) should be allowed to make such decisions for competent patients which go to the heart of our democratic values of autonomy and self-determination, and for incompetent patients which would allow their use as means for others' ends. I want to offer some observations in support of my contentions.

ISOLATION, REPLICATION OF RESEARCH

Research with human beings should be carried on with the minimal number of projects (and subjects) necessary to obtain important scientific results. At present, IRBs work in isolation from other IRBs and, thus, similar experiments are being carried out at countless institutions that often only duplicate studies already in progress. Using human beings unnecessarily, as if they were as readily available as guinea pigs, is, I believe, unwarranted. A *National Human Investigation Board* could orchestrate efforts to keep unnecessary repetitions of experiments to a minimum.

INTERNAL CONFLICTS OF INTEREST

The majority of IRB members are on the faculty of the institutions to which the investigators belong. For example, the IRB at Yale-New Haven Medical Center consists of 26 members of whom 15 are full-time medical school faculty, five others are affiliated with the Medical Center, and four are medical students. The IRB members not only share similar interests and objectives, but they also know, when sitting in judgment of a research protocol, that their proposals may soon be subjected to similar scrutiny. Thus, it is unlikely that members of IRBs will hold investigators to standards that will protect the subjects of research, if doing so would place impediments on the conduct of research and affect the well-being of their colleagues (and eventually also their own well-being) in decisive ways;

ILLEGITIMACY OF "DEFERRED CONSENT"

The evolution of the idea of "deferred consent" is an example in point. It originated at a midwestern medical center, when its IRB was reviewing a research project on head trauma to which patient-subjects could not consent and members of their families were deemed too distraught to give meaningful consent. Eventually the IRB decided that:

Families would be informed at the time of admission that their kin would be entered in an experimental project, but would not be explicitly told that they could refuse, or be asked at that time to consent either orally or in writing. Within 48 hours, however, the investigators would have to obtain written consent from the family to continue the patient in the study…Initial notification gave an opportunity for withdrawal. Such decisions which would essentially compel patients to participate in research without consent and, in addition, could also create guilt feelings in family members for not having listened carefully and then objected to their loved ones' participation in the research.

REVENUES UNDERMINE RESPONSIBILITY

Local IRBs are under pressure, not only from investigators but from their own institutions as well, to approve research protocols. Medical research since World War II has become a research industrial complex. Academic institutions rely on the revenues which accrue from the assessment of indirect costs to the providers of grants. Research proposals have to be generated and completed at a rapid rate to assure future grant support. Thus, investigators are under considerable pressure to recruit subjects as quickly as possible to support the institutions' buildings, laboratories, staff and salaries. With respect to the needs of their institutions, and career advancement, physician-investigators are thus the victims of an institutional system (their own institutions and the National Institutes of Health) which penalizes them for fulfillment of their ethical disclosure obligations toward patient-subjects. These pressures impact significantly on the speed with which informed consent is obtained, and the ways in which the process is conducted, so that patient-subjects will not refuse to participate.

There are other examples of inattentiveness to the informed consent process: the federal regulations on informed consent are in need of a thoroughgoing reevaluation from many perspectives. This is another task for the *National Human Investigation Board.* Most generally, the informed consent requirement should emphasize that taking informed consent seriously in research negotiations obligates physician-investigators to spend considerable time with patient-subjects. They should provide explicit instructions on the lengths to which investigators must go in explaining themselves and their intentions, so that patient-subjects will not be misled.

Physician-investigators need to be cautioned that the requirement of informed consent for research is much more stringent than it is for therapeutic settings. More specifically, the information to be provided in informed consent forms needs to be thoroughly reevaluated. At present they are often incomprehensible, because they are written at a higher reading level than is appropriate for the intended population. Also they include too much distracting technical information of little consequence to the decisions patient-subjects must make. Indeed, at present, subjects are overwhelmed with unnecessary scientific information that clarifies little and serves more the purpose of obscuring crucial information that they need to know.

PRIVATE INFLUENCE

Increasingly, research is being supported by pharmaceutical companies and biotechnical companies with economic rewards accruing to medical institutions and investigators. The conflict of interest problems which such arrangements spawn are troublesome, and they, too, must be examined in depth and regulated by a *National Human Investigation Board.*

These problems are now compounded by the proliferation of so-called free-standing IRBs, which operate outside university settings. Their activities deserve our attention. From what I have learned so far, they are insufficiently regulated. What concerns me

to begin with is that these IRBs are for-profit enterprises and that the owners appoint their ethical review committees who are paid by the owners and serve at their pleasure. In such settings, conflict of interest is surely an ever-present danger. Let me provide one example of anecdotal evidence. Last year, I asked the owner of one such IRB, whom I judged to be a thoughtful and caring person, whether she had ever rejected a research proposal. Her answer was an unqualified "No," and she explained further that she would of course suggest improvements in protocol design, but outright rejection was too delicate a matter.

NATIONAL BOARD

In conclusion, let me emphasize once again, that the Board I envision should have the authority to formulate research policies that seek to resolve the inevitable tensions between the inviolability of subjects of research and the claims of science and society to advance knowledge. Such a Board's proposed policies, of course, should first be subjected to a relentless public debate, and then also approved by Congress. IRBs will still have important functions to perform, but their work will be guided by a National Board to whom they will be held accountable and to whom they can also turn for advice.

The importance of research has captured the imagination of the Western World, and is now being carried forward on an unprecedented scale, and with great expectations of the rewards it can bestow on mankind. Yet, in the quest for progress — the danger is great that deeply held moral values of respect for individual citizen-patient-subjects will be eroded. This may be a price not worth paying. If, as some fear, a *National Human Investigation Board* will slow the pace of medical advances by forcing society to make difficult moral choices in bright sunlight, so be it. I am not convinced that this will happen, but if it does, I believe it is a far better option to embrace than our being corrupted by practices in secret. The recent revelations about the radiation experiments are an example in point.

READING

22

THE FUTURE OF INFORMED CONSENT: AN OVERVIEW

Arthur L. Caplan

Arthur L. Caplan, Ph.D. has worked in the field of medical ethics for more than eighteen years. He is currently Professor of Bioethics and Director of the Center for Bioethics at the University of Pennsylvania.

■ POINTS TO CONSIDER

1. What is an Institutional Review Board (IRB)? Identify some of the criticisms Caplan expresses concerning the current IRB system.

2. Discuss "privatization" of research and the possible conflicts of interest it presents in research with human subjects.

3. Explain the reasons multi-site studies present challenges for IRB oversight.

4. Summarize the author's concerns with respect to persons unable to give informed consent for research.

Excerpted from the testimony of Arthur L. Caplan before the Subcommittee on Human Resources and Intergovernmental Relations of the House of Representatives Committee on Governmental Reform and Oversight, May 8, 1997.

One of the most startling changes has been the shift from public to private sources in the funding of human subject research. Private industry is now the major source of funding for biomedical research in the U.S.

It is time to revisit the adequacy of human subjects regulation in the United States for three reasons: a rapidly changing research environment that casts doubt on the adequacy of informed consent and Institutional Review Board (IRB) review, a lack of basic information about who is involved in research, and inadequate attention to the needs of those who are most vulnerable in research contexts. These reasons provide a basis for a reexamination of human research ethics.

CHANGING ORGANIZATION

For thirty years research in the United States has been subject to policies and regulations imposed by the Federal government. In the wake of scandals in the late 1960s and early 1970s, such as the Tuskegee syphilis study, two sets of protections were created for those recruited to serve as subjects in biomedical research. The first, informed consent, requires that participation in research be voluntary, informed and freely chosen. The second, review by local institutional review boards (IRBs), insures that the scientific merit, risk/benefit ratio and informed consent documents associated with individual research proposals are approved by the peers of those seeking permission to undertake research. Local review with relatively little centralized oversight by Federal agencies of recruitment and consent practices was held to be most consistent with American values, easier to implement and most responsive to the style of Federally sponsored, project- and researcher-oriented funding that characterized biomedical inquiry in this country in the 1970s and early 1980s.

PRIVATIZATION

One of the most startling changes has been the shift from public to private sources in the funding of human subject research. Private industry is now the major source of funding for biomedical research in the U.S. Since 1980, industry's share of U.S. biomedical research and development rose from 31% to 46%, while the National Institutes of Health (NIH) share dropped from 40 to 32%. The dramatic increase of industry funding of biotechnology and clinical research is reflected in university research budgets as well. Industry support of all university research has nearly doubled in the last decade from 4% to 7%. More than a third of the authors of a recent sample of leading biomedical journals had at least one potential conflict of interest as a result of receiving private support or holding a financial interest in the drug or device being studied.

COMMERCIAL CONSIDERATIONS

Access to information for subjects, researchers and the public is emerging as a problem. More secrecy is being introduced in research protocols as a result of the fact that commercial motives are fueling the content and direction of an increasing number of biomedical research projects. Private concerns can and do exercise control over what researchers may publish. When a University of California San Francisco (UCSF) researcher found that a widely used drug Synthroid, which costs Americans $600 million per year, was biologically equivalent to the much less expensive generics, the company suppressed publication of the findings and threatened UCSF with a lawsuit to keep the study from being published.

The privatization of research has led to another shift in human subjects research. Private concerns frequently seek subjects in order to test new drugs or devices they wish to bring to the marketplace. Federally funded research was far less likely to be driven by commercial considerations than is privately sponsored research. This means that human subjects may be asked to carry risks or face the burdens of participation in a research trial not fully understanding that the research is being undertaken with a commercial purpose in mind.

The shift toward more private rather than public support of research raises questions about the adequacy of local IRB review which plays such a key role in the Federal oversight of human research. IRBs may not always know what the conflicts of interest are that exist due to ties between researchers and private funding sources. They may themselves be in a conflicted position, trying to do the right thing by those who are subjects but feeling tremendous pressure not to alienate those who provide the bulk of support for a particular center or department within an institution. Indeed, some forms of research, when conducted entirely with private support, may not fall under the legal aegis of IRB review.

MULTI-SITE STUDY

Today, many subjects in research participate in "multi-site" studies. These are studies that involve many investigators recruiting subjects at many different institutions and locations, often across national boundaries. Multi-site research was not the model that shaped the creation of local IRBs, as the lynchpin of peer review for approving human research. And it is becoming increasingly obvious that local IRBs cannot handle some of the issues that arise in public and privately funded multi-site research. One such example is the large scale misconduct which, in 1994, cast suspicion over the integrity of the *National Surgical Adjuvant Breast and Bowel Project* (NSABP), the single most important source of information women facing surgery for breast cancer have available for themselves and their doctors.

Dr. Roger Poisson of St. Luc hospital in Montreal fraudulently enrolled at least 100 subjects into this study. His patients constituted 16% of the study population. Researchers in this multi-center study were paid on the basis of the number of patients enrolled. High subject recruiters such as Poisson were also given authorship on key papers from the NSABP.

UNDETECTED FRAUD

None of the fraud which occurred in this study was detected and reported by any IRB. In fact, there were tremendous variations in the informed consent forms used by participating institutions to recruit subjects. And no IRB member was ever asked to audit or debrief any subject or investigator in the study at any point during the many years it ran.

Multi-site research poses real challenges for the current system. Indeed, some research is conducted under the auspices of IRBs that are hired for the sole purpose of reviewing studies, raising questions about their ability to assess and monitor local conditions and the needs of particular subjects for information or special protection in particular places.

A LACK OF BASIC INFORMATION

This is not at all unusual. IRBs lack the manpower, budget or time to do very much more than review written research protocols and check informed consent forms. In my experience I have never

met an IRB member who has spent any serious amount of time debriefing subjects or visiting with researchers. They almost never talk with researchers or subjects. Thus, they remain uninformed about the extent to which, what they require on paper in the way of informed consent, is actually put into practice.

Compounding the burden IRBs face is the fact that there is no systematic data collection about the demographics of participation in human research. We mandate far more stringent data collection and monitoring regarding animal subjects than we do for human subjects. If there are trends involving the participation of women, poor people, the mentally ill or Native Americans or any other group, no historical data exists about the nature of those groups involved in human research.

DEBRIEFING, PERFORMANCE CHECKS

Nor is there any systematic debriefing done of those who have participated in research or who have acted as surrogates for those not competent to consent for themselves. This means that IRBs must operate in a vacuum when issues of discrimination, fair access or bias arise with respect to research protocols. It also means that there is no way to check whether IRBs actually do emphasize in their work the kinds of issues that are most important to those who actually serve as human subjects.

Nor is there any systematic data collected on IRB performance. Audits of IRBs are rare and usually triggered by the hint or allegation of a problem. The ability of IRB members to monitor the actual conduct of research and their skill in doing so is not demonstrable by existing means of oversight of the IRB system. Many subjects remain unaware of what to do if they feel they have been mistreated or wronged in the course of research.

VULNERABLE SUBJECTS

For many years it has been well understood that not all subjects in human research can look out for their own interests. When people are, for various reasons, incapable of exercising their power of self-determination, of acting as an autonomous agent, they are at increased risk in serving as a subject because one of the two forms of protection deemed crucial for ethical experimentation, informed consent, is not available to them. Classic examples of such vulnerable subjects are children and fetuses. Special regulations govern their participation in research since they are unable to consent to participate for themselves.

Experiments have been conducted on persons with mental illness where informed consent has been poor and the monitoring of subjects involved in studies inadequate. Complaints by a number of persons afflicted with schizophrenia and their families about studies carried out at the University of California at Los Angeles (UCLA) raise some very tough questions about the adequacy of existing rules for protecting those made vulnerable by mental illness. Issues have arisen concerning the rights and duties those serving the nation on active military service have in times of war and peace with respect to participation in biomedical research undertaken for military purposes. Some of those who served in the Persian Gulf conflict were exposed to vaccines and drugs under circumstances that closely resemble research with no informed consent. And terminally ill persons have been subject to all manner of innovative efforts in clinical therapy.

Those who cannot consent or who can do so only in a limited sense, still deserve the opportunity to participate in biomedical research. There are often benefits to be gained from participation in research, both direct for the subject and indirect in terms of knowledge gained that can benefit others with similar conditions. Vulnerability is not in itself a sufficient reason to deny participation in research to any person. But, there is sufficient evidence available to conclude that some groups, such as the mentally ill, the institutionalized demented elderly and those in military service, require more protection than they are currently being afforded by existing regulations. Others, such as children, the terminally ill and the unexpectedly acutely ill, may need more protection than they are currently being afforded by a system of local IRB review.

BIBLIOGRAPHY

Books - Nazi Medicine

Annas, G. and Grodin, M., eds. **The Nazi Doctors and the Nuremberg Code.** Oxford University Press, New York, 1992.

Berben, P. **The Medical Experiments. Dachau: 1933–1945, The Official History.** Norfolk Press, London, 1975, 123-137.

Beyerchen, A.D. **Scientists Under Hitler.** Yale University Press, New Haven, CT, 1977.

Caplan, Arthur L., ed. **When Medicine Went Mad.** Totowa, NJ: Humana Press, 1992.

Dicks, H. **Licensed Mass Murder.** Basic Books, New York, 1972.

Gallagher, H.G. **By Trust Betrayed: Patients and Physicians in the Third Reich.** Henry Holt, New York, 1990.

Kevles, D.J. **In the Name of Eugenics.** Alfred A. Knopf, New York, 1985.

Lifton, R.J. **The Nazi Doctors – Medical Killing and the Psychology of Genocide.** Basic Books, New York, 1986.

Muller-Hill, B. **Murderous Science. Elimination by Scientific Selection of Jews, Gypsies and Others, Germany 1933–1945** (trans. G. Fraser). Oxford University Press, Oxford, UK, 1988.

Pappworth, M.H. **Human Guinea Pigs: Experimentation on Man.** Beacon Press, Boston, 1968.

Proctor, R.N. **Racial Hygiene: Medicine under the Nazis.** Harvard University Press, Cambridge, MA, 1988.

Shirer, William L. **A History of Nazi Germany.** New York, Fawcett World Library, 1959.

Trials of War Criminals Before the Nuremberg Military Tribunals; The Medical Case. U.S. Government Printing Office, Washington, D.C., 1948.

Books - Japanese Biological Warfare

Brackman, Arnold C. **The Other Nuremberg: The Untold Story of the Tokyo War Crimes Trials.** New York: William Morrow, 1987.

Cole, Leonard A. **Clouds of Secrecy: The Army's Germ Warfare Tests over Populated Areas.** Totowa, New Jersey: Rowman and Littlefield, 1988.

Harries, Meiron, and Harries, Susie. **Soldiers of the Sun: The Rise and Fall of the Imperial Japanese Army.** New York: Random House, 1991.

Harris, Robert, and Paxton, Jeremy. **A Higher Form of Killing: The Secret Story of Chemical and Biological Warfare.** New York: Hill and Wang, 1982.

Hersh, Seymour M. **Chemical and Biological Warfare: America's Hidden Arsenal.** Indianapolis, Indiana: Bobbs–Merrill, 1968.

Montgomery, Michael. **Imperialist Japan.** New York: St. Martin's Press, 1988.

Myers, Ramon H. **The Japanese Economic Development of Manchuria,** 1932 to 1945. New York: Garland, 1982.

Piccipallo, Philip R. **The Japanese on Trial: Allied War Crimes Operations in the East, 1945–1951.** Austin, Texas: University of Texas Press, 1979.

Pritchard, John R., and Zaide, Sonia Magbanua, eds. **The Tokyo War Crimes Trial: The Complete Transcripts of the Proceedings of the International Military Tribunal for the Far East.** New York: Garland, 1981.

Sheldon, Harris H. **Factories of Death: Japanese Biological Warfare, 1932–1945, and the American Cover-up.** New York: Routledge, 1994.

Magazines and Newspapers

Beals, W.B. "The Nuremberg Code." **Journal of the American Medical Association,** 11/27/96, 1691.

Beardsley, Tim. "The Cold War's Dirty Secrets." **Scientific American,** May 1995, 16.

Braffman-Miller, Judith. "When Medicine Went Wrong: How Americans Were Used Illegally as Guinea Pigs." **USA Today Magazine,** March 1995, 84.

Brody, Baruch A. "In Case of Emergency: No Need for Consent." **Hastings Center Report,** Jan./Feb. 1997, 7.

Buchanan, Allen. "Judging the Past." **Hastings Center Report,** May/June 1996, 25.

Coghlan, Andy. "Pioneers Cut Out Animal Experiments." **New Scientist,** 08/31/96, 4.

Davidson, Nestor M. "Sovereign Immunity and the Human Radiation Experiments." **Columbia Law Review,** June 1996, 1203.

Day, Michael. "Third-World Human Lab Rats." **World Press Review,** Sept. 1997, 36.

"DOE Compensates Experiment Victims." **Science News,** 12/21/96, 410.

"Exception from Informed Consent Requirements for Emergency Research." **Journal of the American Medical Association,** 11/27/96, 1632.

Faden, Ruth. "The Advisory Committee on Human Radiation Experiments." **Hastings Center Report,** Sept./Oct. 1996, 5.

Faden, Ruth. "U.S. Medical Researchers, the Nuremberg Doctors' Trial, and the Nuremberg Code." **Journal of the American Medical Association,** 11/27/96, 1667.

Gordon, Danielle. "The Verdict: No Harm, No Foul." **Bulletin of the Atomic Scientists,** Jan./Feb. 1996, 33.

Grodin, Michael A. "Legacies of Nuremberg." **Journal of the American Medical Association,** 11/27/96, 1682.

Harkness, Jon M. "Nuremberg and the Issue of Wartime Experiments on U.S. Prisoners." **Journal of the American Medical Association,** 11/27/96, 1672.

Hentoff, Nat. "The New Tuskegee Experiment." **Village Voice,** 10/01/96, 8.

Hilts, Philip J. "Radiation Tests Used Some Healthy People." **New York Times,** 01/19/95, B10.

Hilts, Philip J. "Radiation Test Secrecy Linked to Lawsuit Fears." **New York Times,** 12/15/94, B19.

Hilts, Philip J. "'Thousands' of Human Experiments." **New York Times,** 10/22/94, 10.

Ho, David. "It's AIDS, Not Tuskegee." **Time,** 09/29/97, 83.

"How to Turn Humans into Guinea Pigs." **New Scientist,** 08/31/96, 3.

"Informed Consent Issue Subject of Case's Remand." **American Medical News,** 07/07/97, 20.

"In Tuskegee Experiment's Wake: Apology, Fellowships and Grants Offered." **Black Issues in Higher Education,** 06/12/97, 8.

Katz, Jay. "The Nuremberg Code and the Nuremberg Trial." **Journal of the American Medical Association,** 11/27/96, 1662.

Kaye, Melissa W. "Tuskegee, Part Two." **Public Citizen,** Spring 1997, 3.

Leary, Warren E. "In 1950's, U.S. Collected Human Tissue to Monitor Atomic Tests." **New York Times,** 06/21/95, B8.

Macilwain, Colin. "U.S. Radiation Reports Fail to Satisfy Critics." **Nature,** 10/12/95, 470.

Macilwain, Colin. "U.S. Radiation Report Prompts Bioethics Move." **Nature,** 10/05/95, 374.

Marshall, Eliot. "Panel Faults Research Consent Process." **Science,** 10/06/95, 25.

Marwick, Charles. "Bioethics Commission Examines Informed Consent from Subjects Who Are 'Decisionally Incapable.'" **Journal of the American Medical Association,** 08/27/97, 618.

McCarthy, Michael. "Cold War Human Radiation Experiments in the USA." **Lancet,** 11/26/94, 1498.

McLean, Sheila. "Commentary: No Consent Means Not Treating the Patient with Respect." **British Medical Journal,** 04/12/97, 1076.

"National Conference on Implementation of the Waiver of Informed Consent in Emergency Situations." **Journal of the American Medical Association,** 08/06/97, 379.

"Officials Cite More U.S. Tests with Radiation." **New York Times,** 02/10/95, A12.

Pace, Brian P. "Panel Discusses Ethics of Studies on Humans – Especially the Poor." **Journal of the American Medical Association,** 11/27/96, 1692.

Preziosi, Marie-Pierre. "Practical Experiences in Obtaining Informed Consent for a Vaccine Trial in Rural Africa." **New England Journal of Medicine,** 01/30/97, 370.

Proctor, Robert N. "Nazi Medicine." **Journal of the American Medical Association,** 04/26/95, 1306.

"Radiation Victims Protest Biased Investigation." **Progressive,** Dec. 1994, 14.

"Research Ethics and the Medical Profession." **Journal of the American Medical Association,** 08/07/96, 403.

Reverby, Susan M. "Everyday Evil." **Hastings Center Report,** Sept./Oct. 1996, 38.

Schwalm, Steve. "FDA Approves Human Guinea Pigs – Sometimes." **Human Events,** 11/22/96, 4.

Shenon, Philip. "Pentagon Cites Radium Risk for Up to 20,000 Ex-Troops." **New York Times,** 08/28/97, A14.

Strosnider, Kim. "Energy Department Will Pay $4.8-Million to Settle Suits Over Radiation Experiments." **Chronicle of Higher Education,** 11/29/96, A34.

"U.S. Conducted Widespread Radiation Experiments." **American Medical News,** 11/21/94, 11.

"Was This Consent Informed?" **American Journal of Nursing,** May 1997, 23.

Wise, Jacqui. "Patients Do Not Read Consent Forms." **British Medical Journal,** 12/07/96, 1421.

"Written Informed Consent Not Necessary." **American Medical News,** 04/14/97, 26.

INDEX